Historical Re

"PERIOD RUSH"

The Cultural Anthropology of Period Cultures

Karol Chandler-Ezell

KENDALL/HUNT PUBLISHING COMPANY
4050 Westmark Drive Dubuque, Iowa 52002

Cover Credits:
Ladies doing needlework (top left) and presentation of heraldry (top right) images © Karol Chandler-Ezell
Civil War reenactment (top middle, background) images © Steve Shore
Archers image © Kristina Hayen

ISBN 978-0-7575-3888-9

Printed in the United States of America
10 9 8 7 6 5 4 3 2 1

Table of Contents

Preface

Goals and Themes of this Book

Historical Reenactors and "the Period Rush": The Cultural Anthropology of Paracultures presents an anthropological look at reenactment groups and the people who participate in them. The book has three objectives. First, this is an anthropological investigation of reenactment groups that explores the activities and motivations of participants. I take a biocultural and adaptive approach to this study, asking "why do people participate in reenacting?" and "what function does it serve?" To answer these questions, I apply sociocultural theories of adaptive behavior, cultural function, and cultural processes to understand the role that reenactment participation plays for individuals. Society for Creative Anachronism, Renaissance Faire, Civil War, and other reenactment groups are described and discussed. The groups are compared and contrasted to the Society for Creative Anachronism (SCA), the reenactment group where I began my investigation. This comparative approach is used to point out both the similarities and differences in the groups. Though the SCA and other medieval European groups are not the most common or oldest of the reenactors, as the first group I investigated, they are the standard to which I began to compare other groups.

Second, this book allows me to present information gathered during my dissertation research into the use of herbal remedies by Americans. In my search for individuals using and practicing traditional European herbal medicine, I found that many people were using and studying traditional or folk medicine as a part of historical reenactment activities. In particular, many members of the Society for Creative Anachronism (SCA) were very knowledgeable about medieval European medicine. Many of the experts I initially discovered actually suggested I come to reenactment events and meetings to watch them in action and meet other informants. In this way, I learned that the rediscovery and sharing of historical knowledge is a very important part of reenactment culture. In order to access and interview herbal medicine use, I needed to do ethnographic work with historical reenactment groups. Many of the herbal practitioners and consumers I interviewed were involved in alternative groups and had multiple social connections to historical and/or fantasy reenactors even if they themselves, did not participate. The underlying network of social connections was linked through the reenactment and other social groups, not the herbal knowledge use itself. I began by studying the culture of herbal remedies and ended by learning that herbal remedy knowledge was actually a manifestation of deeper cultural movements like establishing and maintaining a connection to historical, cultural, and environmental heritage. Use of herbal and other alternative medicines by these people was more of a symptom of social problems and unmet needs in American culture that people were solving. As I tried to learn more about reenactors and better understand how they were connected to my dissertation topic, I realized that these groups were largely unstudied. This book is an attempt to share the world of paracultures and the people who inhabit this realm.

Third, *Historical Reenactors and "the Period Rush": The Cultural Anthropology of Paracultures* illustrates the ethnographic and ethnobiological research process. I use this book and the topic of reenacting to illustrate anthropological and social concepts of culture's adaptive nature and how cultural movements are shaped by peoples' needs.

I have written this book to be accessible to undergraduate students and beginning graduate students in the social sciences as well as those who have an interest in reenactment groups. I hope that it will also interest professionals and more advanced graduate students interested in social movements, social psychology, and culture change.

Organization

The book is arranged in four parts. Part I provides an overview of the project as well as the research design and theoretical concepts used to understand reenactment groups. Part II describes reenactment groups. Part III compares the different groups and revisits the theoretical concepts, placing the reenactors in a larger context to demonstrate what they reveal about culture and our social needs. Each chapter has a set of suggested assignments or activities students may use to learn more.

Acknowledgements

I would like to acknowledge the people who have contributed to this work and without whom this book would not exist. First, I would like to thank all of the reenactors who gave generously of their time and knowledge. They welcomed me and brought me into their world. Kristina Hayen served as my guide into the SCA, introducing me to the art of "playing" and other reenactors, undertaking my initial enculturation, and even hosting me at events. My gratitude to the many other gentle folk of the kingdoms of Calontir, Meridies, Ansteorra, Outlands, and Middle, especially those of the Stronghold of Forgotten Sea, the Shire of Standing Stones, and the Barony of Three Rivers for their hospitality and generosity. I would like to thank Thomas Ezell for being my guide and contact for Civil War reenactors. He went to investigate living history presenters, as a favor to me, while I was working on my dissertation research and found brotherhood, friendship, and a most satisfying way to relieve stress. I thank Deborah Pearsall, my doctoral advisor, for her support and enthusiasm as the importance of reenactment groups became more apparent, as well as her patience and guidance through my doctorate and dissertation. I would also like to thank my dissertation committee for their support and contributions to the initial research: Robin Kennedy, Louanna Furbee, Kathryn Coe, and Gery Ryan. Each provided unique and invaluable support. Peter Gardner for long talks about sacred time, role reversal, and the importance of paracultures. Catherine Chmidling, Suan Rickabaugh, and Shanna Francis accompanied me on fieldwork and along with Alex Chandler-Ezell, Thomas Ezell, and

Michael Dietz spent many hours reviewing numerous drafts of this project. I thank my colleagues at Stephen F. Austin State University's Sociology Department for their support and contributions through discussions and reviews on this text: Peggy Moss, Diane Dentice, Mark Frazier, Jerry Williams, Ray Darville, J.B. Watson, Bob Szafron, Jerry Tyler, and Tom Segady. Finally, I would like to thank the editors and staff at Kendall-Hunt for their patience and support in transforming a dissertation into a book. Special thanks to Stephanie Ramirez and Ryan Schrodt.

Part 1

Cultural Anthropology & the Study of Reenactors

Why Study Reenactors? Issues That Shaped the Research

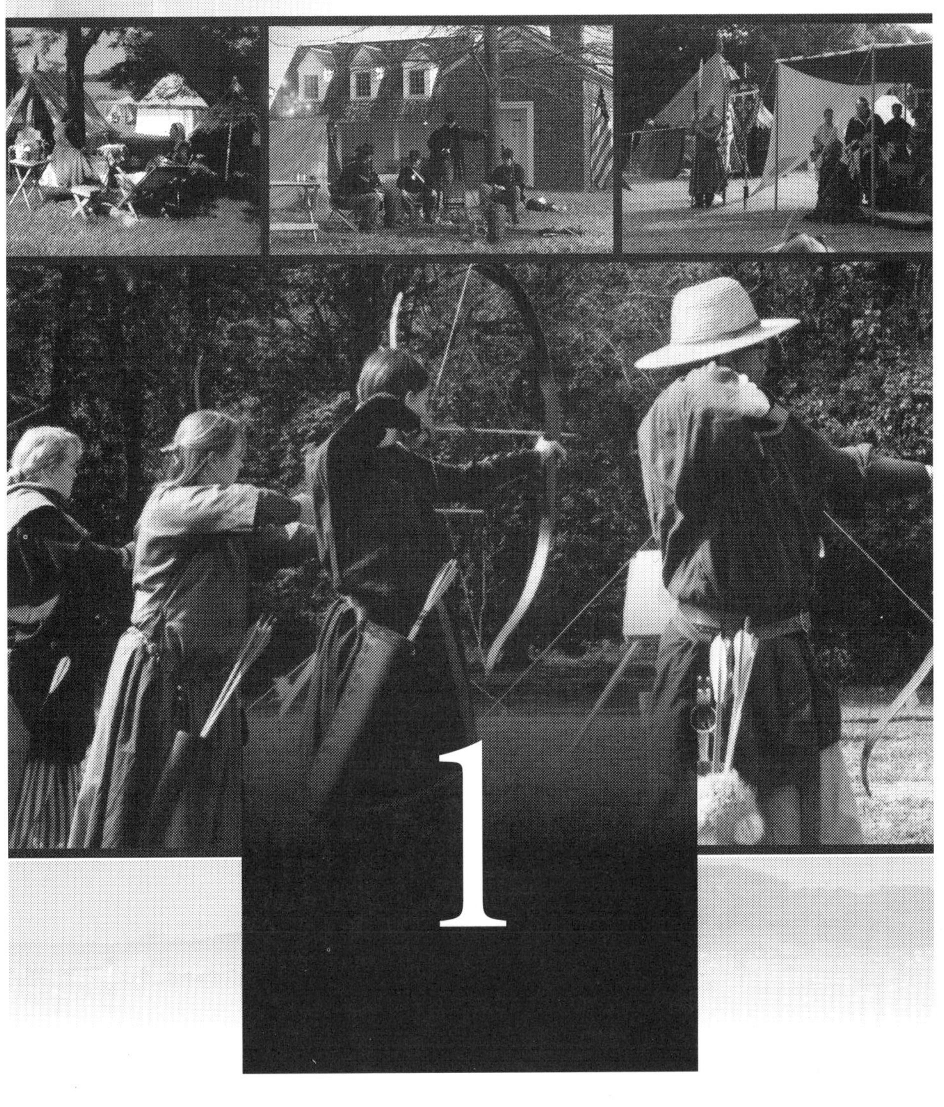

1

What Are Reenactors?

The topic of this book is reenactors and their cultures. Reenactors are people who act out characters and events from a particular historic period or event. They are hobbyists, but the term *hobby* often fails to capture the amount of time, effort, and detail invested in many reenactors' re-creations. Much time is spent researching the time period to be enacted, especially the customs, clothing, accessories, grooming, and historical details. A reenactor works hard to construct a **period** (historically-accurate) **persona**. They spend a great deal of time learning history and culture to create and develop their persona, which is often subject to peer review by other reenactors.

Reenactors are different than people who merely wear a costume for an event like a party or an entertainment job. Unlike actors or the casual party-goer, reenactors do not wear costumes. The historic clothing, accessories, and grooming they use are designed to help them to get into character, as a part of a form of method acting where they try to experience the reality of the time period. Whereas a person wearing a costume is aware that they are wearing something which is fake, the reenactor attempts to become the person who makes the costume real clothing. This is why many reenactors are often angered by comments about their "costumes", when they are, from their viewpoint, wearing their uniform, **garb**, finery, etc... Calling their painstaking recreation a costume accuses them of fakeness and often even jars them "out of the moment", ruining the experience of reenacting for them. Those accustomed to living history performances, by contrast, have learned to interpret such questions as genuine expressions of interest and incorporate them into their narrative and educational activities. Simply using a word other than "costume," such as "uniform" (military reenactors), "garb" (medieval reenactors), or just "clothing" (most reenactors consider this an acknowledgement of the "non-costume" role) to compliment a reenactor's hard work will often please a reenactor and elicit a stream of enthusiastic explanation of their persona and the research and effort they have invested in the details of their appearance.

The time period chosen for reenactment is usually a matter of personal preference (an enthusiasm for a particular time, culture, or event), convenience (what reenactment groups are accessible to the hobbyist), and cultural heritage. The most common reenactment genres in the United States are Civil War, Revolutionary War, European medieval/renaissance, and Rendezvous. Growing in popularity are other military reenactment periods such as World Wars I and II, Vietnam, and Korea. World Wars I and II, the Roman/Greek period, Bronze/Iron Age Celtic, and the Napoleonic Wars are very popular reenactment genres in Europe. In the U.S., Canada, Australia, and Scotland, Scottish Highland living history is very popular, especially by descendants of the Scots who either emigrated or were transported after the battle of Culloden. Colonial-type genres are very popular in the United States and Canada, with enthusiasts reenacting early colonial life, Lewis & Clark, the Old West, Cowboys, early settlers to the West, and Spanish Colonials. Rendezvous, in particular, is a popular genre in Canada, the Northern U.S., the Midwest, and the Smokey Mountains which focuses on fur trappers and mountain men from the 1750s–1840s in the Americas and is quite different from military-oriented reenacting from the same time period. In Texas, the Spanish-American War, the War of Texas Independence, the

American Civil War, and Texas Republican reenactments are popular. There are even Pirate reenactors in the Caribbean and along the southeastern U.S. coast.

Medieval and Renaissance reenacting includes both Renaissance Faires and groups like the Society for Creative Anachronism, which are quite different despite their shared time period. The Society for Creative Anachronism, started in Berkeley, California in 1966, has spread to Canada, United Kingdom, Sweden, Finland, Germany, Italy, Greece, Romania, Japan, New Zealand, South Africa, and Australia. The S.C.A. currently (as of 2006) has about 30,000 paying members, with many more people who participate in local events without joining the official organization, and is probably the single largest reenactment organization. In sheer numbers by genre, American Civil War reenactors are estimated to number anywhere from 40,000–60,000, but these are spread among many different individual organizations. In this book, I focus on the genres with which I have had the most interaction: the S.C.A., Renaissance Faire, and Civil War reenactors.

Though this book focuses on historical reenactors, there are a great number of people who enjoy fantasy reenactment. **Fantasy reenactors** seek to enact non-historical realms or universes. Common fantasy genres for reenactment are those from comic books, fantasy worlds, horror, science fiction, and RPGs (Role-Playing Games). Star Wars and Star Trek are particularly popular genres for reenactment. Because fantasy reenactments do not have the anchor of historic locations, they often occur in settings such as science fiction/fantasy conventions, gaming sessions, and online environments. It is interesting to note that while many reenactors pick a single genre, be it historical or fantasy, some reenactors enjoy multiple genres of reenacting, depending on their mood.

Negative Misconceptions About Reenactors

Most people in the United States and Canada have heard of reenactors, particularly of Civil War reenactors and medieval European reenactors like the Society for Creative Anachronism (S.C.A.). To outsiders, these activities are often viewed as very marginal or "weird." When I mention that I've researched reenactors, people's responses range from neutral ["Why do they do that?"] to positive ["Wow, I'm glad someone is keeping the history alive"] to the negative ["Aren't those guys a little nuts?"] Context seems to be an important factor here: reenactors are a fun addition to museum events and heritage festivals, but they are often mocked if people encounter them in everyday life. Other people have even more negative impressions of reenactors that should be addressed and dispelled in order to let the reader approach the subject with an open mind.

Nostalgia and White Supremacy

A common misconception about American Civil War reenactors is that they are white supremacists, motivated by racism and nostalgia for a past when whites dominated all other races. The most negative and prevalent accusations against Civil War reenactors are those of racism and white supremacy. In "*A Century of Civil War Observance*," John Hope Franklin (1962) said that Civil War observances, from flags to parades to plaques, were "unworthy of the vaunted American goal of freedom and equality." His argument was that Negroes (African Americans) may no longer be slaves in legal terms, but they were certainly not yet full and equal citizens with the rights and freedoms of other Americans. Because of this, Franklin held, the Civil War was a failure. He was particularly critical of early reenactments that were taking place in the centennial remembrance of the war.

> *"Sham battles are being staged to stimulate the imagination and to encourage viewers to second-guess the outcome." (pg 104)*
>
> *"Why is it that a mature, somewhat sophisticated, and indisputably powerful nation would subject itself to ridicule before the entire world with the vulgar reenactment of the Battle of Bull Run?" (pg 104)*

People who object to Civil War reenactment on the grounds of racism associate the Civil War simply with slavery and white supremacy. Many African Americans, in particular, are offended by what they see as glorification of the Confederacy and the Southern antebellum period which practiced slavery. To these individuals, the Confederate Battle Flag, Confederate uniforms, and remembrances of the Civil War seem like a celebration of white supremacy. This is reinforced when such symbols are proudly displayed and used by actual white supremacist groups such as the Ku Klux Klan. To be specific, people who object on these grounds object to portraying *Confederates* from the Civil War as anything but slaveholding villains. They are all right with movies or reenactments that portray Southerners as ideological caricatures of evil slaveholders. In short, Southerners are the bad guys. In the deep South, by contrast, Union soldiers are often the boogeymen, appearing as ominous characters in local folklore.

The image of General Sherman still reminds Southerners of the brutal Atlanta Campaign. Copyright Jupiter Images.

The problem with this is that it ignores that the Civil War was about much more than slavery. Franklin himself explains that he is upset not that the Civil War was being remembered, but that it was memorialized in an overly simplistic way that ignores its true significance. He holds that the Civil War was the unifying national experience of the United States and should be remembered in that way. His point is that the Civil War and Reconstruction experience was the furnace that forged a new, unified United States and Americans with a shared national identity, regardless of which side of the war our ancestors chose. Because of it's salience to our cultural identity, it is natural that we would have a great interest on this conflict and time period. Civil War reenactment groups are focused on this goal. They seek to experience this time when our national character was forged and then communicate that to their audience. Their research is both a personal quest to discover what it was like to actually be in the shoes of the people they are memorializing and to make sure that the lessons learned in the War Between the States are never forgotten. In anthropological terms, they seek to gain an insider's, or "emic" perception, through participant observation.

In their own words:

> *"The Nineteenth Century Living History Association and its subsidiaries are volunteer organizations dedicated to the serious research, study, preservation, and accurate description of persons and events of the American Civil War, both Union and Confederate. Furthermore, the various Corporations and its Board of Directors denounces racism, racial supremacists, hate groups and other groups or individuals that misuse or desecrate the symbols of the United States of America and/or the former Confederate States of America; and has no modern political agenda or status." http://www.texas-brigade.com/frmain.htm*

Most of these groups also require that members be willing to portray either Union or Confederate soldiers as needed to make the most realistic reenactments. Some travel to events with the paraphernalia for two alternate characters just in case.

Brothers in arms wearily return to camp after a long day reenacting the Battle of Shiloh.
Photo by Steve Shore

The greatest argument against inherent racism in Civil War reenactment is the popularity of African American reenactors. While the popular film *Glory* brought attention to the African American soldiers who fought for the union, a more recent documentary by Stan Armstrong is *Black Confederates: The Forgotten Men in Gray.* African Americans participate in Civil War reenacting, portraying people from both the Confederate and Union sides.

Yet another consideration is the cultural importance of the Antebellum period, the Civil War, and Reconstruction for Southerners. In the South, Civil War reenactors are viewed as stewards of Southern culture and spark a personal nativistic connection in people who feel personally connected to the Civil War. Many southerners know Civil War stories of their great-grandparents and other relatives. Civil War historic sites and artifacts of the Antebellum period saturate the Southern landscape. The Antebellum period serves as the dawn of civilization for the south. It is viewed nostalgically as a fairy tale time, romanticized as peak of culture and beauty for many, particularly as it is portrayed in the media. In contrast to this, the destruction from the war and Reconstruction were times of hardship and poverty which the South endured much more than the North. The Southerners were the only Americans who've ever been invaded, conquered, and occupied on their home soil. (Though the Native Americans experienced this, they were viewed as "Other" by European-descent colonists.) The horrors of the war and the long decades of poverty which followed made the Antebellum period seem even more romantic by contrast. The Civil War provided regional legends and folklore from the dawn of Southern culture. The signs and symbols of the war, especially the Confederacy, are associated with the great deeds of ancestors for many Southerners, and it is difficult for many to forget this even when they know those same symbols are painful to others. As a result, while others may have negative perceptions of Civil War reenactments, they are often very positively viewed by Southerners.

This sort of culture clash will continue as long as characters from the war are simplistically viewed as good guys and bad guys in particular regions. The goal of living history is to actually breathe life and complexity into these characters by portraying them in a realistic way. By portraying "real" people with complex motivations and personal histories, reenactors do much to dispel simplistic stereotypes of the people who lived through the Civil War. Their fantasies and playacting are done to teach a more realistic perspective on the war.

"Get a Life" and "Grow Up"

Other reenactors are often accused of immaturity, or a failure to differentiate reality from fantasy. While there have been reenactors that were psychologically unwell; they are rare, and this is simply not true for most reenactors. There are two major reasons for the belief that reenactors are unable to discern fantasy from reality.

First, the assumption is that if reenactors are "just playing", then they must be immature. Playing dress-up and wearing costumes is seen as a childish activity in our society. It is neither productive nor normal adult behavior, so it is frivolous. Many of the crafts and skills that reenactors learn take a great deal of practice and research, yet they are often viewed as esoteric or outdated. While some outsiders are excited and enjoy seeing that someone is preserving knowledge of older times, investing so much time and often money in a craft that is today carried out much more quickly by machines is often viewed as extravagant. The very lack of efficiency and the imprecision characteristic of handmade items or older technology is prized by reenactors and living historians for its uniqueness. Even a crookedly stitched costume is proudly displayed to other reenactors as a product of their own hands. It is well received as a sign of the willingness to learn and try despite setbacks by other reenactors. Stories about the mistakes and difficulties one has learning an old craft, especially the creation of garments, is a common topic of friendly chatting and socializing among reenactors. Eventual mastery of these skills gains the reenactor prestige and higher social status amongst his peers. Classes, workshops, and study groups on older skills, crafts, and knowledge make up a large portion of reenactor interactions and activities. Social sharing of knowledge, experience, and materials is a method of bonding and integrating people into the reenacting community. A new recruit's first activity with the group is working with other reenactors to learn how to create the material artifacts (especially clothing) needed to portray their new alternate persona. As they help mentor the new recruit in material culture, the more experienced members of the community also establish friendships and pass on the social aspects of their culture.

Second, if outsiders accept that reenactors are playing seriously, they then assume that it is a sign of aberrant psychology. Most of the scholarly writings on reenactors make a point of diagnosing reenactors with Fantasy-Prone personalities and even personality disorders or defects. Their conclusions assume that mature, psychologically healthy individuals do not play act. This ignores the ubiquity of ritual role-playing in human culture. Anthropological research shows the importance of rituals and role-playing. Rituals are basic cultural mechanisms for communicating identity, ideology, and camaraderie as well as for acting out significant cultural events. Victor Turner's research into the function of rituals shows the importance role-playing for alleviating stress, forming social bonds, and experiencing **communitas**.

Weird Is Beautiful to the Social Scientist

The very wealth of misconceptions about reenacting makes it an interesting anthropological topic. The general goal of people within a society is to be viewed as **culturally competent**. This means knowing the social rules and norms and being able to successfully fill accepted social roles. People who do not manage to maintain a socially acceptable role frequently suffer anxiety and social stigma in addition to endangering their status and success. It can be socially dangerous to be an outsider. Anthropologists and other social scientists study marginalized people or groups of people for a variety of reasons. Common research questions about

SCA fighters battle for the Crown, Crown Lists Tourney in the SCA Kingdom of Calontie, 2001
Photo by Karol Chandler-Ezell

marginalized groups include trying to understand why a group becomes marginalized; how their social status affects their mental and physical health; how to improve their access to educational, economic, and health resources; and what their social dynamics are.

Whether it is viewed positively or negatively by outsiders, reenacting is definitely viewed as doing something that is outside the norm. Marginalizing yourself by doing something that makes you noticeably ***deviant*** (outside normal range of behavior disregard) is socially risky and may negatively affect your social status. Participating in reenacting is merely socially dangerous—there are usually no serious risks of being physically harmed in modern Western culture, but it is noticeably outside the norm and causes people to react and view the reenactor as deviant. Why, then, do people take this social risk?

That is what this book hopes to answer. The simplest answer is that reenacting fills a social and psychological need. The experience of reenacting and the social atmosphere of being part of the reenactment community gives participants something that they do not get out of their everyday, mainstream lives. The following chapters seek to demonstrate how those needs are filled.

As stated in the Preface, I take a cultural and adaptive approach to this study, asking "why do people participate in reenacting?" and "what function does it serve?" By using sociocultural theories of culture change and adaptive behavior, we can begin to understand the important and adaptive role that reenactment participation plays for individuals. Revitalization Movements and Invention of Tradition, two important sociocultural theories which apply to nostalgic culture processes, are discussed in Chapter 2. In the following chapters, the Society for Creative Anachronism, Renaissance Faire, Civil War, and other reenactment groups are described and discussed. The groups are compared and contrasted to the Society for Creative Anachronism (SCA), the reenactment group where I began my investigation. This comparative approach is used to point out both the similarities and differences in the groups. Finally, we return to the questions of how sociocultural theory sheds new light on much of the reenactment phenomenon.

Name ______________________________ Date ________________

Activities

Survey Common Perceptions of Reenactors

List the types of reenactors you had heard about before this book.

Go back and score your impression of each type of reenactor as positive or negative. Then, describe your initial impressions of each type of reenactor. After you've read the chapter, use the last column on the right to mark whether your opinion was changed.

List types of Reenactors	Initial Impression? + | −	Describe your initial impressions of each type of reenactor	Opinion changed? + | −

Name ______________________ Date ______________

Now go and survey your friends or family. Ask them to list any types of reenactors they know. Ask them their impressions. Then ask them if they've actually seen any of those reenactors.

List types of Reenactors	Initial Impression? + | –	Describe your initial impressions of each type of reenactor	Have you ever seen this type of reenactors? Where?

Follow-up

Compare your list to the ones you gathered from your friends and family. How do they compare or differ?

____

____

____

How do their opinions compare to your own?

____

____

____

Name ______________________ Date ______________

Do you think you have a sample that is representative of most Americans? Explain.

How do you think opinions might vary in other areas of the country?

Short Answer/ Brief Essay Questions

1. What are some common *negative* impressions people have about reenactors? Do you think that these have merit? Explain.

2. What are some *positive* reactions people have to reenactors? What social factors contribute to positive reactions instead of negative ones?

3. What types of reenactors do you expect to develop in future years? Explain.

Anthropological Theory and Research

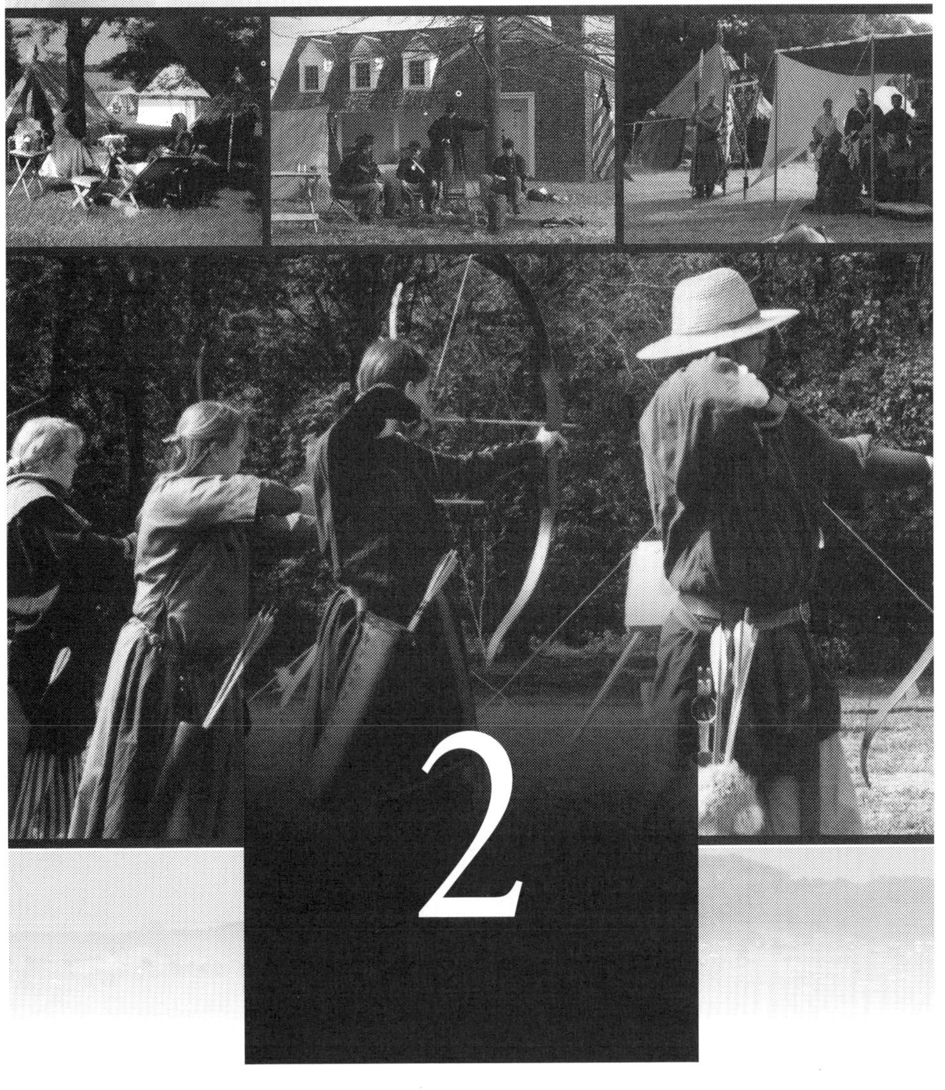

2

Ethnographic Studies: How Anthropologists Study Living People

The study of culture is the basis of cultural anthropology, also known as **ethnology**. The root "*ethnos*" comes the Greek for "people", and is used to refer to a culture. Ethnology, then, is the study of people, particularly what makes them "a people", or society–their culture. Many other fields study people, but both the methods and approach used in anthropology set it apart from other fields of study focused on humans and their activities.

The anthropological approach is *holistic*, seeking to integrate multiple aspects of the human experience, including the biology, history, psychology, and social and physical environments of experience. Anthropological research is conducted through fieldwork, or gathering data from a naturalistic setting instead of a laboratory. People are studied in their natural social and physical environments, not in a laboratory. The methods anthropologists use in studying people include cross-cultural comparisons and the ethnographic method. An **ethnography** is a writing about a people or culture from an anthropological perspective. It is the product of an ethnographic study. Doing ethnographic fieldwork is the process of discovering, studying, and describing a people as you are among them. Part of the professional training of a cultural anthropologist is learning to conduct ethnographic fieldwork.

Ethnographic methods include observation, especially participant observation; interviews; life histories; surveys; censuses; taxonomies; language catalogs; and kinship studies. The anthropologist takes on the role of a student or sometimes even a child as they learn what it means to be a member of a society. In the early days of anthropology, young ethnographers were sent to study "their people", usually a fairly small group of non-Western, non-Industrial people who were considered "primitives." Today anthropologists study groups of various sizes and are increasingly studying complex societies.

Subcultures, Microcultures, and Paracultures: Studying Complex Societies

As someone who takes an adaptive approach, I am interested in investigating counterculture movements and subculture patterns. In particular, I am interested in how people cope with stressors from their environment, health, and culture's pressures. Subcultures are groupings of people within a larger culture that define coherent, separate groups of individuals sharing a culture: i.e. history, language, religion, identifiable badges, and practices. Examples of subcultures include Hmong immigrant communities in Canada or Cajuns in Louisiana. While subcultures exist at many levels, they are coherent systems, classified hierarchically as a smaller unit within a larger culture. Members of subcultures are fully integrated into that culture either by enculturation from childhood or by the process of joining the group.

Anthropologists working in complex societies are beginning to focus more on even smaller divisions of social groups. In very large societies, even subcultures may be very large, with a large and diverse membership that would be difficult to fully study in a holistic and complete ethnographic study. One way to make smaller studies more feasible, is to work with microcultures. **Microcultures** are smaller social categories with specialized knowledge and customs. They differ from subcultures that they do not define a whole way of life (McCurdy et al. 2005). Microcultures tend to be associated with one aspect of members' lives, such as their occupation, recreational groups, and other activities. People within a microculture share a set of behaviors, specialized language, and knowledge. Some typical examples of microcultures include firefighters, college sororities or fraternities, sports teams, surfers, and many more groups you encounter daily. Microcultures are useful for understanding slices of a larger culture, especially particular contexts of daily life.

Despite their similarities to microcultures and subcultures, historical and fantasy reenactors differed in several qualitative ways. Reenactor culture are not as large as subcultures, and reenactors are still members of different and larger subcultures. Reenactor culture is not just a microculture either, because the transitions between participating in mainstream culture and participating in reenacting culture with an actual alternate persona exist in parallel. People transition between the two, but keep them as separate identities within themselves, choosing which is the outward social identity at different times.

Renaissance garb appropriate for SCA or Ren Faire. Copyright Jupiter Images.

When actively performing a reenactment, the everyday self is submerged and replaced by the alternate persona and culture. If participants in alternative cultural groupings like reenactment groups are actually moving periodically back and forth into this parallel culture instead of converting fully to members of stable full-time subcultures, they are better described as being part of a **paraculture.** ***Para-*** in this usage refers to the paraculture being both parallel and outside or in tandem to everyday culture. Paracultures are tightly knit groups such as historical reenacting which make their hobbies intense, shared "cultures" that saturate much of their daily life and self-identity while operating parallel to mainstream life. Members of paracultures are distinct in that they "slip into" an alternate role from the paraculture. Cross-cultural studies show that the practice of temporarily taking on alternate social roles is common to many societies and allows social freedom to perform rituals, escape social pressure, and mitigate stressful situations. I argue that members of paracultures take on alternate personas as a way of coping with psychological and cultural stress and that it is an adaptive behavior designed to meet people's underlying needs, fears, and even perceived threats to their health and well-being. Studying paracultures allows us not only to learn the specialized practices of a cultural grouping but also can provide insight to the stresses from the larger culture with which people are trying to cope.

Cultural Mechanisms for Creating New Subcultures: Revitalization Movements and Invented Traditions

Two anthropological concepts which are mechanisms of culture change and synthesis of new subsystems. Both revitalization movements and inventions of tradition are methods by which cultures may adapt to better meet the needs of individuals within a culture. Both concepts offer insight into how reenactment culture grows and develops as well as to why individuals participate. Together, the two concepts introduce a theoretical and anthropological way of viewing reenactment culture.

Revitalization Movements

Introduction to Revitalization Movements

Revitalization movements are cultural processes by which an alternate paradigm for a cultural subsystem challenges and replaces the current mode. A paradigm is a framework or model for understanding and thinking about a particular area of thought, especially for a body of knowledge. The dominant paradigm is the most prevalent or influential model people have for how a particular body of knowledge or part of a culture works. In order for culture to change, paradigms have to change as well, so these dominant paradigms are periodically replaced by new or updated paradigms. It can often be difficult to change people's minds, so paradigm changes are often accompanied by many debates and competition between people who subscribe to the dominant paradigm and the new, alternate paradigms being proposed. The cultural subsystem paradigm under debate could be a religious, medical, or even a costume system.

Because they are part of paradigm change and revision, revitalization movements are an integral step in the development and change of cultures from internal forces. Instances of revitalization had been known since early anthropological studies, but Anthony Wallace's (1956) unique grouping and modeling of revitalization movements changed the way anthropologists view both religion and cultures themselves. Although the most frequently studied aspect of revitalization movement is the process of replacing old systems for new, many revitalization movements actually result in the failure of the new system to be accepted. Instead, a reinvented, new-and-improved version of the old system or paradigm results. Revitalization movements are more about incorporating new or newly revised cultural elements that are more in tune with the current cultural needs of a people than wholesale replacement. This repeats periodically, in a process that lets cultures undergo adaptive reinvention, editing, and updating. Close study by Wallace showed that revitalization movements are actually cyclical, with three distinct phases in a cycle that repeats at differing rates depending on need due to stress within a culture. To learn more about revitalization movements, the concept of revitalization movements in the anthropological literature is reviewed first, then the factors behind and the traits typical to such movements is discussed.

It was Anthony F. C. Wallace who first assigned the term "revitalization movements" to provide a generalized terminology for a whole class of sociocultural phenomena involving deliberate attempts to innovate cultural systems (Wallace 1956, 1966). Most anthropological literature investigates the social process of religious revitalization movements. Indeed, revitalization movements are often religious phenomena, as people seek to reform a whole society from within through changes in religious beliefs and customs. Classic examples of revitalization movements include Melanesian cargo cults, the Mau Mau of Kenya, Mormonism, the Branch Davidians, and many movements among North American Indians, such as the Ghost Dance, the Peyote Cult, and the Handsome Lake Religion. Current examples of religious revitalization movements include American Neo-paganism and Modern Pagan Witchcraft.

It was Wallace's work with revitalization movements from the 1950s-70s that promoted them from cultural curiosities to a major process of culture-change. Wallace developed a theory of revitalization process with two major points. First, Wallace claimed that ***all*** the major religions—including Judaism, Christianity, and Islam—and their branches actually sprang from revitalization movements. Revealing the mechanisms of revitalization movements as integral to the birth and development of major religions made them one of the most important processes in shaping cultures over time. Before Wallace's work, revitalization movements had been seen as cultural novelties brought about by then-recent stresses like the European acculturation of "primitives." Secondly, Wallace described revitalization movements not as one-time events, but rather as stages in a regular, consistent cycle of cultural progress. The impact of Wallace's theory was strengthened because he also presented cross-cultural evidence documenting a uniform process for cycles of cultural change including these phenomena. It is the unification of revitalization movements into a single class, with an overall mechanism incorporated into a functional explanatory model of culture change that sets Wallace's work apart from earlier studies. Revitalization movements, according to Wallace, are a crucial step stage in an endless cycle of cultural processes. Since the adoption of Wallace's model, he and other anthropologists have explored many examples of revitalization movements. Revitalization movements, as described by Wallace and those who followed him, are now an accepted tenet of basic anthropological theory.

Before Wallace

In the early writings of anthropology, the "sophistication" of a society's culture and religion were used to rank its overall development and degree of civilization. Early writers in anthropology like Sirs Edward B. Tylor (1832–1917) and James Frazer (1854–1941) were unilineal evolutionists, believing that cultures and religions progressed upwards to increasing sophistication. In this view, cultures (and their religions as a part of their culture) moved slowly upward through a linear progression beginning in savagery and barbarism and culminated to its peak in the "sophisticated" Western civilizations. In this view, all cultures were slowly moving and progressing forward but non-Western cultures were perceived as less advanced and definitely inferior. Cultural progression under this model was distinctly linear.

Franz Boas (1858–1942) and his many students introduced historical particularism into anthropology. In this new Boasian anthropology, "primitive" cultures were largely static, and their cultures were not seen as progressing at all, much less in a line or cycle. Studies of revitalization movements during these times considered to be separate events and defined by their specific, or "particular," cultural characteristics. They were considered different phenomena, each unique to their culture. Studies like Mooney's 1896 text *The Ghost Dance Religion and the Sioux Outbreak of 1890,* which described the classic revitalization movement among the Sioux in detail, were definite products of the Boasian tradition of cultural particularism, though the data from Mooney's book was reinterpreted and used by many scholars since. The Boasian tradition emphasized understanding a particular culture and set of events as unique, not as a process common to other situations or culture. Documents and studies from this period did not unify revitalization movements as a class, but they have been useful because they have provided valuable ethnographic information for later studies. Wallace, LaBarre, and those who followed them in studying revitalization movements fruitfully used studies from the Boasian period and before in order to perform cross-cultural comparisons and illustrate more generalized cultural processes.

Despite the fact that both of the early anthropological traditions utilized linear models of culture change, this early ethnographic work is still usable for reevaluation under the cyclical process model of Wallace. Both of the early traditions held culture change as a "gradual chain-reaction effect", a "slow, chain-like, self-contained procession of superorganic inevitabilities (Wallace 1956)." The result is that though Revitalization movements were recognized, they were seen as instances along that chain where rapid, momentous change occurs.

The influence of Freud and psychology in anthropology led to studies aimed at understanding *why* different types of revitalization movements took place. Scholars from the Culture and Personality era of anthropology such as Mead, Barnett, Linton, Williams, Smith and Wallis were all discussing different kinds and aspects of revitalization movements in the decade prior to Wallace's model. These studies directly influenced Wallace and he discussed and acknowledged them in his landmark 1956 paper in which he described his model of revitalization processes, then went on to show that their work was subsumed by his new theory.

Wallace credits H. G. Barnett's, 1953 book, *Innovation: the Basis of Culture Change,* for its focus on acceptance and rejection of cultural innovations. The focus on the processes by which cultural innovations are either accepted or rejected was important to Wallace's model. He was also influenced by Margaret Mead, who a paper read at the 1954 annual American Anthropology Association meeting, detailed her study of nativistic movements (revivals of native culture in reaction to acculturation stress) via systems theory. Just a year later, Mead stated that cultures could and did change just in the span of a single generation.

Wallace grouped the different aspects of these processes studied by other anthropologists into a group, or "class" of revitalization-type units and put their work together to better understand how these processes worked and how they were alike or dissimilar. He started by looking to the work of other scientists to gather a full range of the many forms of these movements. For example, Linton specifically looked at **nativistic movements,** which were a response to negative acculturation. The goal of nativistic movements is to reject alien elements from the culture in an attempt to purify and reinvigorate cultures (not just to change or replace the culture as other revitalization movements do). Even though Linton's research focused on a single type of revitalization movement, his work paved the way for Wallace's work. In particular, Linton proposed that cultural development moved forward and backward along a line of development. This was a new idea, since the dominant paradigm in anthropology before Linton was that culture was an ever-progressing straight line, with an emphasis on progress and forward development. While Linton's model was just a change to horizontal movement between two points on a line, the repetitiousness of the process foreshadows Wallace's model of cultural processes that are cyclical and also repeating but never going "backwards".

Wallace incorporated ideas and work from many other early anthropologists as well. From James Mooney's "revivalistic" movements, Wallace takes the idea of instituting cultural elements, customs, and values lost from an idealized past. From Williams and Whitehead, Wallace added millenarian movements and cargo cults, a counterpoint to Linton's nativistic movements in that they imported the alien elements actively. From Wilson Wallis came much work on prophet figures in Messianic movements.

Wallace credited the ideas and theoretical advancements in the work of all of these scholars for influencing his theory. What Wallace did with the field of culture change and process, however, unified all of these pieces into a coherent whole. Wallace stated that all of the phenomena such as millenarian movements, cargo cults, nativistic movements, and Messianic movements were merely different types of a universal cultural process. He termed this class of phenomena "revitalization movements" and set about describing a systematic model focused on process. Wallace's model of revitalization movements provided the hows and whys these earlier anthropologists had been seeking. It also transformed the loosely grouped category of revitalization process into a unified and widely applicable model for understanding a variety of phenomena as local variants of a universal process.

Wallace's Model

Cultural stresses give rise to revitalization movements. The types of cultural change phenomena that arise are usually a mixture of several processes and depend on the cultural stresses provoking the movement. In Wallace's model, any particular type or mixture of types of the revitalization phenomena (cargo cults, Messianic movements, etc . . .) was possible. By accepting the different types of revitalization phenomena as variations on a theme, all with the same goal of relieving the stress felt by individuals within the society undergoing change, Wallace was able to simplify his model. The influence of Sigmund Freud's ideas from psychology and systems theory is obvious in Wallace's solution to organizing and clarifying the previously confusing and incoherent cultural phenomena as a people trying to cope with stresses in their social environment.

A revitalization movement, then, as articulated by Wallace, is **"a deliberate, organized, conscious effort by members of a society to construct a more satisfying culture."** The important phenomenological point in revitalization movements is that the individuals involved see their culture or parts of it (often, their religion) as a functional system. These parts, or subsystems, must also function. When they fail to function to the satisfaction of the people within the culture, they need to be repaired. People realize that they must change individual elements as well as the overall structure of the system, and they deliberately set out to build a new system which is better adapted to their present and future needs. It is the deliberateness and explicit nature of the attempt to update their culture that makes revitalization movements stand out in culture change. People within a revitalization period advertise and promote the need for change as well as their solution.

Wallace, as others in the 1950s before him, treated the revitalization movement as a response, an intentional emic adaptation of culture. Revitalization is the process by which the people within the society are responding to the pressures exerted by their environment, both biological and nonbiological. As such, it is an adaptive strategy for cultural evolution.

To better understand how revitalization movements can help societies survive, it is important to understand how Wallace viewed the function of culture and religion in societies. Religion and culture serve a vital function in a society. Culture, as a whole, is a society's extrasomatic, or nonbiological, means of adapting to the environment. It provides individuals within a society with "a design for living that helps mold responses to different situations" (Fagan 1997). In that context, a society's religious system, then, is the spiritual framework in the culture which helps individuals both psychologically and socioculturally. This explains why religious structure and change are so often studied by social scientists and why so much of the theory uses religion as its example. Other elements of culture besides religion provide people with cognitive or philosophical framework for coping psychologically and socioculturally, however, including the social connections people in paracultures like reenactment groups. These ideas and the anthropological theories about how they work are used in this study

SCA reenactors study details from texts, tapestries, and stained glass art to create authentic reproductions.
Copyright Jupiter Images.

because they have the common function of providing a functional model for behavior and belief.

In the Freudian- and systems theory- influenced anthropology of the 1950s, the rituals and experiences in a religion are part of the system which heals the discomfort and anxieties caused by various stressors, provides models for solving conflicts, and integrates individuals into a community. The myths and religious lore of a society provide models of coping for resolving conflicts, and the religious complex includes central values and behaviors that the individuals within a society need in order to integrate the varied parts of that society (Wallace 1966, Whitehead 1969). Cultural systems give individuals identities and placements within the structure of that system. People know where they fit within the system and how they relate to the world as long as their religious and cultural systems maintain a good adaptive fit to their environment.

The functions of religion and culture are exposed when stressors or shifts in the culture's environment change the needs of the society and expose failures in the current system. Common stressors preceding revitalization movements are political revolution, climate change, economic decline, civil war, culture change (such as technological innovations or an influx of new individuals), population decimation, invasions, and acculturation (see scholars like Linton 1943, Wallace 1956, 1966, La Barre 1970, Kehoe 1989, Haviland 1997, Kimbrough 1995). All of these stressors change the environment within which the cultural system (and its religious subsystem) functions. Inevitably, the now poorly adapted culture fails to meet all of the needs of the people within that society. These people begin to experience anxiety from uncertainty and the lack of a coping model within their cultural or religious system. They don't know how to act, what to do to improve the situation, or how to successfully manage. The society may decline, especially when in competition with other cultures. There are various adaptive coping strategies available to those within a society. One common solution is to consciously innovate their religious and cultural system into a new, better adapted model.

Wallace's Cycle of Adaptiveness

After studying the Handsome Lake religion among the Seneca of the Iroquois, Wallace saw a pattern to the processes of revitalization. He was able to look at the hundreds of examples in anthropological literature and see common themes. He saw revitalization movements as adaptive phenomena instigated by members of a society to retool, or refit, their culture so that it would be better adapted to their physical, biological and cultural environment. Of especial importance to anthropologists is the conscious nature of the revitalization phase. The other phases of Wallace's cycle do not show this intense self-awareness, sometimes even to the point of the individuals within the society being unaware of the adaptive function of their culture.

Wallace's cycle is different in that it was the first to truly be a cycle, not a chain or line with only two points, or states. Instead of the old idea of a progressive linear development, cultures and their subsystems were moving through time with an ever-responsive functional process. Wallace proposed that culture is not directional or linear, as believed by Tylor and Frazer. It is not static, as treated by Boasian anthropologists. Instead, culture is adaptive, changing, and often cyclical. Wallace's cycle can be seen as a constant flow from **stabilization** to **decline** to **revitalization** (Figure 2.1).

Cycle of Revitalization Movements

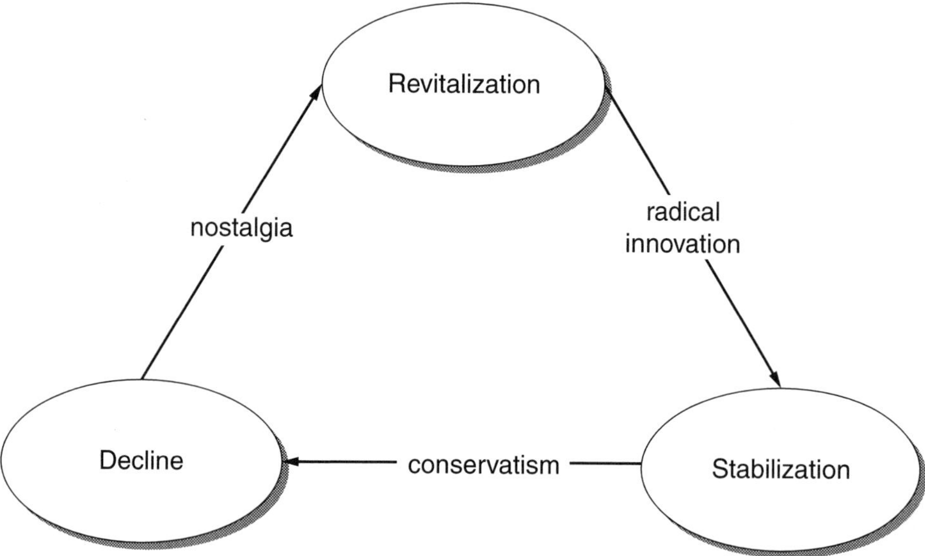

Close examination of the three phases shows how the actions of a society reveal an attempt (sometimes consciously and sometimes unconsciously) to maximize the fitness of the system. The period of stable culture occurs when the society's cultural models are well adapted to their environment, allowing them to function and prosper in relation to their surroundings and neighbors. Stressors reduce the adaptiveness of their system, and a period of decline begins. The decline worsens until the society (or a portion of it) is threatened by their failure to function successfully. At this point, the society is ripe for a revitalization movement.

The revitalization period is typified by the intentional and conscious adaptation of the cultural subsystem to the perceived needs of the society's members. When a revitalization movement takes hold and successfully manages to innovate a new, better adapted system, stabilization begins. The stabilization period, in contrast to the revitalization period, is typified by a very conservative maintenance and codification of the newly adopted system. This helps to cement the new system into place. At this phase, any competition from alternate paradigms is vigorously avoided. This conservatism slowly shifts to nostalgia during the period of decline as members try to cling to the remnants of their tattered system. The liberalism and radical nature of the revitalization movement is necessary to loosen the hold of the entrenched structure on the past. Ironically, the separation from the entrenched system and a long-held pattern is to call for a move to an even more distant past. Often, the revitalization movement actually promises a return to the glory days of the distant past, nostalgically idealized and beloved system. The movement may even incorporate some of the symbology and ritual of the past. It is important to remember, though, that though the symbols are nostalgic, the system is newly innovated and is not actually a return to the paradigm of the past.

The Processual Structure

Wallace's (Wallace 1956, 1966) model breaks down the progression of steps that initiate the revitalization process. I have summarized his stages as follows:

I. **Steady State:** Most individuals within the population have their needs met. While some are under intolerable stress, they can be dealt with within the system without seriously disrupting others or the steady state of the system. Changes may and do occur, but they are integrated and do not upset the balance.

II. **The Period of Increased Individual Stress:** The individuals within one or more of the system's subpopulations experience stress with increasing frequency and intensity as the culture's efficiency and efficacy at satisfying individual needs both get worse. Many types of agents may interfere with the culture's efficiency, including; among others: changes in physical or biotic environment; military or political defeats; acculturation; economic distress; population fluxes due to epidemics, and migration.

III. **The Period of Cultural Distortion:** The individuals within the culture respond differently to stressors, and do not apply a uniform system. As a result, the culture warps, or distorts. The variety of coping mechanisms employed increases factionalism within the culture. Responses may include symptoms like alcoholism, ambivalence, infighting, abandonment of mores, and a variety of mental disorders. Various groups may make the system incoherent or piecemeal by trying to apply different, or alternative, pieces of behavior to "patch" the system. Mass disillusionment with the mazeway, or increasingly convoluted and increasingly nonfunctional system, increases the stress on individuals and the overall society. If a revitalization movement does not succeed, the period of cultural distortion may end in the death of the society.

IV. **The Period of Revitalization:** The culture is usually in a state of disarray, and has severe problems meeting the needs of individuals within the society. In many cases, it is on the brink of complete destruction from increasing problems stemming from the period of cultural distortion. Usual symptoms may include factionalism, epidemics, starvation, alcoholism, unemployment, and poverty. These problems may be solved or even forestalled by successful revitalization movements.

Within Stage IV, the period of revitalization, there are a series of predictable steps within the process.

1. **Mazeway of reformation:** Both the elements and the subsystems of the cultural system are restructured into an internally consistent structure. The mazeway, or path to reformation, is often dramatic, occurring first in a prophet or leader who brings others into conversion in a rapid, enthusiastic movement. The leader's gestalt insight is often a divine revelation or inspiration. Hallucinations, dreams, meetings with supernatural beings, and visions of the future are the usual method of revelation. An apocalyptic problem is seen in broad overview, alongside a plan for restructuring society and averting the destruction of the prophet's people. The newly reborn prophet is often quite changed in personality and becomes a messianic figure with missionary intent. For examples of the dramatic conversion of revitalistic leaders, see the literature on such prophets as Handsome Lake, Jack Wilson, George Went Hensley, and John Slocum.
2. **Communication:** The visionary must then successfully reveal his revelations to people as a evangelist in order to become a prophet. He or she must convince listeners that the new way will do two things: protect and provide material benefits to both the individual and the culture.
3. **Organization:** Converts pick up the message with enthusiasm, often even with hysteria. The prophet must organize a structure to the new movement, often with deputies (disciples) to distribute the message to the wider base of followers . The structure must facilitate the spread of the message, provide a structure to shaping a new lifeway, and keep the movement going.
4. **Adaptation:** The reconstruction includes local adaptation to the everyday needs and function of the system. The new system as a whole must work, in general and in the particulars, for the newly converted society. In a pattern of feedback, the prophet often readjusts the message to find a better and better fit with the society. The new system grows and innovates until the fit is maximized.
5. **Cultural Transformation:** The new system takes effect as it is applied, reducing stresses and pressures on the individuals within the society. The better the adaptive fit and application of the system is, the better it serves it's newly restructured culture's individuals and overall society.

6. **Routinization:** The new system spreads and integrates into the overall cultural system and daily life of individuals. It's application becomes routine, and conservative forces hold it into place.

Stage V: The New Steady State

Once Stage IV is complete, the fifth and "final" stage begins and is maintained until the process is ready to begin again. The period of innovation ends, and a period of stabilization sets in, as the society attempts to hold steady the new system.

Summary

Wallace's classification and modeling of revitalization movements is accepted and taught in anthropology courses today as basic theory. As it stands, it provides valuable insight into the processes that shape culture in general and religious movements in particular. Many anthropologists since Wallace have studied revitalization movements under Wallace's model, and it has stood the test of time. The goal of current research in this area seems to be to work out the nuances of the model. Recent studies (Anderson 1991, LaBarre 1962, 1970, Kehoe 1989, McLoughlin 1994) try to determine why revitalization movements took particular forms. The end goal is to have an understanding of the model that is not just interpretive but also predictive. After all, if Wallace's model is accurate, revitalization movements are a part of every culture and every religion, past and present. From the dawn of Christianity, Judaism and Islam to the Korean shaman dances of 1998, revitalization movements are born every day, often with tremendous cultural impact.

Wallace's model is used in this study as a way of investigating and understanding the factors in the reenactment participation. Why do people join these alternative cultural groups? They are definitely participating in alternate paradigms of how people behave. The number of people involved in various types of reenactment have grown and participation seems to be holding steady, despite a general lack of acceptance by mainstream American culture. As several different types of reenactors are described in later chapters, they explain in their own words why they join alternative cultural groups. Prominent among their reasons, just as predicted by Wallace's work with revitalization movements, are a need for social participation and acceptance not available to them in mainstream culture and finding ways of coping with sociocultural stress that suit their personal needs.

Invention of Tradition

Introduction to Inventions of Tradition

The concept of invention of tradition is used to describe phenomena which societies (from the state-level down to social clubs) use to apply the authority of time-honored tradition to cultural practices that are actually recent in origin. There are two categories of invented traditions. The 'tradition' in question may either be 1) the product of a discrete, purposeful invention, or 2) a self-establishing yet recent practice. The concept is quite useful, not only for realizing that appearances of long-time tradition may be deceiving with many ritual-heavy cultural institutions, but also in pinpointing society-perceived needs for cultural structure.

Eric Hobsbawm (Hobsbawm and Ranger 1983) is credited with developing the term and concept of 'invented tradition'. In his definition, 'invented traditions' are practices which attempt to establish continuity with the past via new practices falsely given credit as being quite old. Invented traditions differ from other forms of culture change, innovation, and addition in that they are dishonest about their true origins. Unlike myths, which are also frequently ambiguous or dishonest about their credited origins, invented traditions are used to change cultural structure and performance. Regardless of whether they are invented as a discrete event or develop within a short, nondiscrete time period, invented traditions always claim time-honored authority.

The linkage to the past is necessary for the invented tradition to fulfill its function. The function of these practices is to repair a functional or consistency problem within a society's culture. Hobsbawm describes invented traditions succinctly as "responses to novel situations which take the form of reference to old situations, or which establish their own past by quasi-obligatory repetition" (Hobsbawm and Ranger 1983: 2) In other words, the invented practices are cultural adaptations designed to be integrated into the structures of the cultures undergoing functional stresses and stabilize them. The functional stresses could be the problems created by changes, especially rapid or unexpected changes, that leave members of the society without a way of coping with novel situations. A new practice that provides appropriate behavior to the new stimuli is invented or emerges through innovation then spreads and gains popularity. If that practice is viewed as completely new or is not consistent with associated cultural practices, it may cause as much stress as the original disruption. Invented traditions, however, are designed to convince members of society who perform them that they invariable, a form of continuity with the past that helps to stabilize the overall cultural structure.

Because invented traditions stabilize cultures undergoing functional stresses, they are often invented purposefully by governmental institutions, religions, and other authority figures such as political, religious, or commercial leaders seeking to cement and maintain their power structure. Carefully constructed or implemented invented traditions allow old institutions, like universities, governments or the Catholic Church, to maintain their stability to cope with novel situations in a manner that seems consistent. In addition, the new "traditions" appeal to people attempting to establish the validity of alternative paradigms or attempting to resist cultural change they perceive as threatening. Recently invented practices are repeated often to ensure that they are properly absorbed. People tend to forget the recent origin of invented traditions fairly rapidly (within a few years or a single generation) because they are oft-repeated and become common knowledge, unconsciously performed through habit. Because of the way societies remember, the new tradition replaces older ones because it is explained during the enculturation process as 'the way it's done' and often becomes

Artwork of royalty and knights provides inspiration for SCA garments and accessories period. Copyright Jupiter Images.

established (and its recent origin lost) in a single generation (Connerton 1989). A truly successful invention is a practice that blends so smoothly with the past or meets the functional need so well that its recent origin is quickly forgotten. For example, the very "American" holiday of Thanksgiving with turkey, dressing, and family values is cited as a holiday originating in from early celebrations between English pilgrims and friendly east coast Native Americans in the 1600s. Children in our elementary schools are taught about Thanksgiving, usually with plays or stories containing "traditional" pilgrims from the Mayflower wearing black and white clothing and "Indians" who give the new settlers pumpkins, turkeys, and maize. This most traditional of American holidays, however, was actually invented and instituted in the 1863 by President Abraham Lincoln in order to increase a sense of American nationalism and family values during the stressful times of the American Civil War. Sarah Josepha Hale, the editor of *Godey's Lady's Book,* a prominent women's magazine, worked tirelessly to promote and "invent" the Thanksgiving tradition as we know it today. In addition to the countless letters she wrote to every official she could think of (including and especially the President of the United States), Hale published articles about Thanksgiving rituals, foods, and "tradition." Hale was largely successful. Ask any American child (and most adults), and you will get the pilgrim story. A more classic example used in the development of Hobsbawm and Ranger's theory of how inventions of tradition function, however, is the invention of the Highland kilts of Scotland (Trevor-Roper *in* Hobsbawm and Ranger 1983). In particular, the clan-specific and short, distinctive kilt we think of today as a badge of Scottish national identity was actually a much-later 'tradition' born as protesting response to Scotland's forceful Union with England that transformed the Scots' badge of barbarism into the badge of national pride.

Inventions of tradition differ from revitalization movements in several ways. First, they are discretely created and distinctly discontinuous with their supposed historical sources instead of being re-interpretations of actual cultural subsystems. The second difference in the functional level of the two items. Revitalization movements tend to be re-emergences of *concepts* and *beliefs* while invented traditions are *practices* designed to provide support and consistency for systems of belief. Inventions of tradition are actually the tools used by the proponents of competing dominant and alternative factions in the first four stages of revitalization movements. The dominant paradigm or institution uses invented traditions to attempt to cope with the cultural fracturing that emerges when people are dissatisfied with the current system. The competing paradigm uses invented tradition to give their movement the appeal of consistency, validity, and continuity with an idealized past in order to attract more people away from the dominant paradigm and onto its side. For example, as cited above, Scottish nationalists used plaids as badges to assert their own history and nationalism in the face of acculturation by English culture after their political assimilation into the British Empire.

Proponents of both paradigms realize that cultural systems must 1) meet the functional and perceived needs of the people within the society and 2) do so in a fashion that provides people the assurance of stability. A revitalization is the *process* by which a society updates the *culture* as a whole so that it is a robust, cultural system for framing and coping with the world environment. Invented traditions are one of the *tools* with which this is done. While the revitalization process is usually the way in which an alternative or subordinate paradigm gains and cements the position of dominance, inventions of tradition may be used by either the alternate or the dominant paradigm.

While inventions of tradition have the dimension of practice, it is important not to forget that they also have the dimension of justification. The cited distant historical source of the practice is its authority, much in the way that a reference citation in a manuscript uses the older, published reference cited as the authority, or "proof" of the validity of a statement. The ability to convince people within the society of their validity determines whether or not an invented tradition will be successful and durable.

While invented traditions can occur singly, they frequently occur in clusters of several closely-related practices. This is particularly true of institutions under great pressure to establish their validity. Often, smaller movements which fulfill only one cultural subsystem form close associations with other small movements with similar belief systems. The close interrelationship of Modern Pagan Witchcraft and Modern/Eclectic herbalism is an example of such an alliance (Hutton 1999). Both of these counterculture movements trace their roots to pre-Christian or at least pre-Industrialized Northwestern Europe. Both movements seek a closer connection with nature, domestic healthcare and a more female-centered view of history. Both are inconsistent with the other elements of Western culture. By forming an alliance, a complex integrating Paganism and Modern/Eclectic herbalism offer greater stability across cultural subsystems and make these movements more sustainable and comfortable for their practitioners. Similar clustering of invented traditions and revival of older traditions and practices is frequently seen among reenactors. For example, reenactors often learn a great deal about the history and cultural practices of their chosen reenactment genre and incorporate aspects not just from the clothing and hairstyles that are readily apparent to outsiders, but from multiple dimensions of that period into their daily and reenacting lives, including undergarments, accessories, culinary dishes or techniques, toiletries, traditions, music, and more. This gives participants a richer, more holistic experience. For most reenactors, the "costume" is not a façade and is much more than skin deep. They are often quite happy to discuss the skills, technology, philosophy, and even politics of their chosen period.

Name ______________________________ Date ____________________

Assignments

Learning More About Ethnography

Choose an ethnography (you can choose one from the list below or another, as instructed by your professor.) Read the ethnography and write a summary, taking care to note the following things:

1. Author's name and training.
2. When did the fieldwork take place?
3. Who, what cultural group was portrayed in the ethnography?
4. Was this a culture? A subculture? A microculture? Explain how you determined this.
5. Where in the world is the group studied?
6. Describe the culture briefly in terms of their economy, subsistence strategy, political system, religious system, marriage patterns, and other cultural structures as described by the ethnographer.

Your instructor may have you complete a second part of this assignment after you complete Chapters 3 and 4 of this book.

Learning More About Revitalization Movements

Choose one of the following revitalization movements requested:

Revitalization and Nativistic Movements:
The Ghost Dance
Handsome Lake Religion
Cargo Cults in Melanesia, Pacific Islands
Rise of the Ku Klux Klan
Terre sans Mal migrations in South America
Hitler and National Socialism in Germany
Gorbachev and perestroika in the Soviet Union
Ayatollah Khomeini in Iran
Peyote and Native American Church
Black Nationalism in the United States
Falungong

For the movement you chose, find the following information:

Information Search:

1. Author, ethnographer known for studying this movement
2. What were the ***dominant paradigm*** and ***alternate paradigm*** in the movement?

Name ______________________________ Date ____________________

3. The people and culture involved in the movement
   A. The leader, or prophet starting the movement
   B. Supernatural vision, prophecy
   C. What the followers wanted
   D. Are there "bad guys" in the story?
4. The situation that prompted the revitalization movement
5. How did it turn out?

Learning More About the Invention of Traditions

Assignment 1

You may be assigned to either answer these questions yourself or to use them as interview questions to poll other people about this topic.

1. How do you define "tradition?"
2. Describe 3 traditions that you (and perhaps your family) find to be very important. Describe how each of these traditions are meaningful to you and your family.
3. How long do you think something has to be practiced to become a "real" tradition?
4. Is it really important to you to have the exact and accurate historical facts about a tradition, or do you like the standard cultural version? Discuss the pros and cons of each.
5. What is the difference between an "invented tradition" and one that evolves over time without "invention?"
6. What do you think of political powers or corporations inventing traditions?

Assignments: Chapter 2

To learn more, try one or more of these ethnographies:

Benedict, Ruth. 1946. The Chrysanthemum and the Sword: Patterns of Japanese Culture.

Chagnon, Napoleon. 1984. Yanoamo: The Fierce People. (Case Studies in Anthropology) Wadsworth Publishing.

Evans-Pritchard, E. E. 1937. Witchcraft, Oracles, and Magic among the Azande.

Fernea, Elizabeth Warnock. 1969. Guests of the Sheik: An Ethnography of an Iraqi Village. Doubleday.

Mead, Margaret. 1928. Coming of Age in Samoa: A Psychological Study of Primitive Youth for Western Civilisation.

Malinowski, Bronislaw. 1922. Argonauts of the Western Pacific.

Name ______________________________ Date ____________________

Mooney, James. 1900. Myths of the Cherokee.

Mooney, James. 1965. The Ghost Dance Religion and the Sioux Outbreak of 1890. University of Chicago Press.

Quinlan, Marsha B. 2003. From the Bush: The Front Line of Healthcare in a Caribbean Village. (Case Studies in Anthropology) Wadsworth Publishing.

Rappaport, Roy A. 1984. Pigs for the Ancestors: Ritual in the Ecology of a New Guinea People. Yale University Press.

Turnbull, Colin M. 1988. Forest People. Peter Smith Publisher.

Assignment 2: Invention of Traditions

Research one or more (as assigned by your instructor) of the following invented traditions. Who or what agency "invented" the tradition? What is the tradition and/or how is the tradition celebrated? Try to discover the tradition or practice that was replaced by the newer, invented tradition. In some cases (older seasonal holidays, new traditions have replaced older ones).

Holidays: Think of typical customs, special foods, colors, and symbols associated with the holiday.

The "Hallmark Card Holidays": Mother's Day, Grandparents' Day, Bosses' Day, St. Valentine's Day

Patriotic, National, and "bank" or "post office" Holidays: Memorial Day, Labor Day, Veterans' Day, President's Day, Thanksgiving (American and Canadian), VE *Day (note what day of the week these traditionally fall upon)*

Religious holidays: especially Christmas, Easter, All Saints Day

Seasonal holidays: End of Year, Solstices and Equinoxes, May Day, Halloween

Customs:
Pastel colors for babies
Blue for boys, pink for girls
Scottish clan tartans and kilts
Greeting cards/holiday cards
White wedding dresses
Wedding cakes
White before/after Labor and Memorial Day

Learning More About Ethnographic Literature

The Human Relations Area Files is a massive database of ethnographic information from around the world. First compiled and organized by George Peter Murdock in

Name ______________________________ Date ____________________

1937 on library-style index cards, the HRAF is now a massive electronic database available on the internet at http://www.yale.edu/hraf.htm. If your university has a subscription to access the database, you can search through over 800,000 pages of text and images from over 365 cultural groups around the world. Even if your university does not have access to the database, you can learn much by using the public information available on the HRAF website.

If you have full HRAF access either online or through a copy at your university library, you can search the database for a variety of cultural elements and patterns, including the revitalization movements and cargo cults discussed in the chapter.

Information Search 1: Exploring the HRAF

Review the material on the HRAF website and answer the following questions.

1. Why were the HRAF created?
2. What sorts of documents were used to compile the HRAF?
3. What is an OWC code? List them.
4. How are the cultures organized? Describe the levels of classification
5. What is the OCM? How is it used?
6. How are the OWC and OCM codes useful when you are using the database?

Information Search 2: Finding Information on the HRAF Database

Your instructor will give you a culture. Find it's OWC code and write it here ________.

Go do the complete collections list and record what documents are available from that culture. Record the following information:

1. The number of documents in the database _______
2. The number of pages of text available __________
3. The time period these documents cover ___________

Research Design: An Overview of the Project

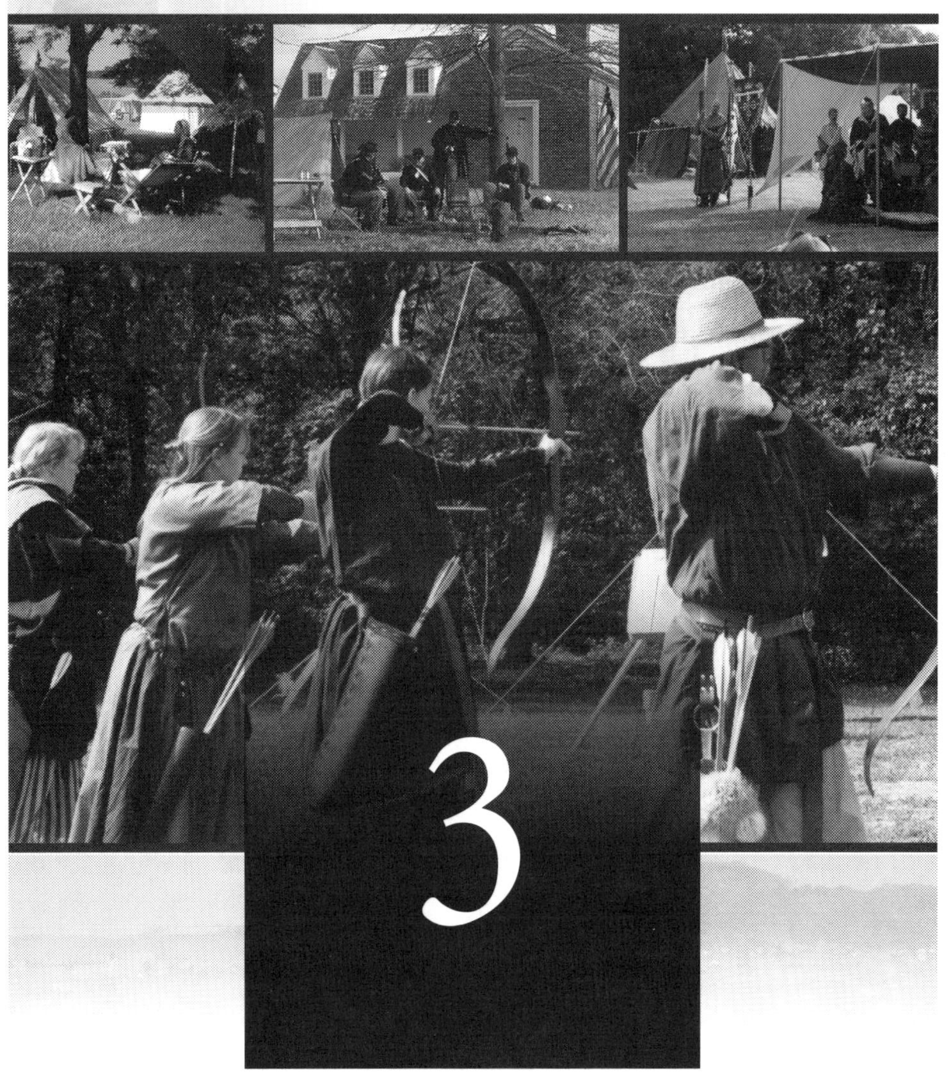

3

As said in the preface, this book allows me to present information gathered during my dissertation research into the use of herbal remedies by Americans. In my search for individuals using and practicing traditional European herbal medicine, I studied historical reenactors. In the process, I became more and more interested in reenactment culture as I learned more about it. Though I began by studying the culture of herbal remedies, I ended up being drawn into an investigation of reenactment culture. Most of my fieldwork was with members of the S.C.A., but curiosity and cross-cultural comparison led me to investigate and interview members of other reenactment genres as well. The following chapter describes the research population studied to provide interview data for this project as well as the environment of that fieldwork.

Research Population and Sample Terms

The first section includes information about the people interviewed as consultants for the study. Generalized information for about the research, or sample, population includes definitions of grouping terms and information about the sub-cultural affiliations of the sample group. Background information for consultants includes their demographic information, affiliations, and the sampling method by which they were identified for interviewing. Next, the environment and setting of the interviews is described; and lessons learned from the fieldwork are described.

Consultants vs. Informants

While individuals interviewed by ethnographers have traditionally been called **informants,** there are problems with this term. While the term *inform* may be defined as to "notify, apprise, enlighten, and advise," and is generally used in this way in the anthropological context, it is also used to mean to "accuse" and, "incriminate" (Abate 1997:pg 406). The term *informant* is defined in the Oxford Desk Dictionary and Thesaurus (Abate 1997) as one who "informs against or on" and is synonymous with the terms "stool pigeon" and "tattletale." The negative associations with the term informant have led many anthropologists to choose alternative terms with less negative associations (Bernard 1995). When speaking with my sample populations, I referred to them as "**consultants**", a term with more positive connotations. The term consultant is also used within the body of this text.

Sampling Structure

The sampling structure is displayed in Tables 3.1 and 3.2. A total of 42 consultants were interviewed, subdivided into: 1) 10 herbal practitioners and 17 herbal consumers from the herbal remedies research project, and 2) 16 additional reenactors who were not selected as herbal remedy consultants. Consultants were assured anonymity, so their names were replaced with anonymous codes identifying their groupings and an individual number. Additional data was gathered from participant observation, observation, informal conversations, and literature review.

Table 3.1. Consultants originally chosen for interview for herbal remedy use, but who identified themselves as reenactors. "Practitioners" are experts who practice as herbalists. "Consumers" are people who consumed at least 3 types herbal remedies regularly.

Groupings	Expertise	Anonymous Code	Gender	Age Group	Sample Context
Practitioners	European herbal medicine	PE02	Female	40–45	S.C.A. event, self-identified
	”	PE03	Female	50–55	S.C.A. event, rec by other expert
	”	PE04	Female	25–30	Rennaissance Faire, self-identified
	”	PE05	Female	30–35	Rennaissance Faire, self-identified
	Modern/Ecclectic herbal medicine	PM01	Female	35–40	rec by consumer
	”	PM03	Female	45–50	self-identified, alternative bookstore
	”	PM04	Male	40–45	rec by practitioner
	”	PM07	Male	50–55	Alternative bookstore, self-identified
	”	PM08	Female	35–40	Alternative bookstore, rec by consumer
	”	PM09	Female	35–40	S.C.A. event, rec by consumer
Consumers	nonexpert	C10	Female	55–60	S.C.A. event
	”	C11	Male	30–35	S.C.A. event
	”	C12	Male	50–55	S.C.A. event
	”	C13	Male	50–55	S.C.A. event
	”	C15	Female	25–30	S.C.A. event
	”	C19	Male	35–40	Rennaissance Faire
	”	C20	Female	30–35	Wiccan coven
	”	C27	Female	20–24	Alternative bookstore, Wiccan coven
	”	C29	Male	35–40	Rennaissance Faire
	”	C30	Male	45–50	Rennaissance Faire
	”	C31	Female	30–35	Alternative bookstore
	”	C33	Female	50–55	S.C.A. event, rec by practitioner
	expertise in herbal medicine	CE06	Female	30–35	self-identified, Wiccan coven
	”	CE07	Female	25–30	S.C.A. self-identified
	”	CE08	Female	25–30	self-identified, Wiccan coven
	”	CE14	Female	40–45	S.C.A. event
	”	CE16	Female	35–40	S.C.A. event

Table 3.2. Additional consultants interviewed about reenactment participation and culture.

Anonymous Code	Gender	Age Group	Sample Context
SCA01	Male	30–35	S.C.A. event
SCA02	Male	25–30	S.C.A. event
SCA03	Male	30–35	S.C.A. event, Rennaissance Faire
SCA04	Female	30–35	S.C.A. event
SCA05	Female	45–50	S.C.A. event, Rennaissance Faire
SCA06	Female	40–45	S.C.A. event
RNF01	Male	40–45	Rennaissance Faire, Rendezvous
RNF02	Female	30–35	Rennaissance Faire
RNF03	Female	20–25	Rennaissance Faire, S.C.A.
RNF04	Female	18–20	Rennaissance Faire
RNF05	Female	18–20	Rennaissance Faire, S.C.A.
RNF06	Female	20–25	Rennaissance Faire, S.C.A.
RDV01	Male	50–55	Rendezvous
CW01	Male	45–50	Civil War, living history
CW02	Male	40–45	Civil War, Rendezvous
CW03	Male	45–50	Civil War, Texas Republican

Experts and Nonexperts

An important pair of terms utilized in cultural research is "Expert" and "Nonexpert". These terms are commonly used in domain analysis to separate sampled populations into two, comparable categories. **Experts** are those that have extensive knowledge of a ***domain*** (area of knowledge) and are recognizable by their training, credentials, or even their ability to extensively and authoritatively use knowledge from that domain. Experts, quite simply, know more about a particular type of knowledge than nonexperts. These categories are highly useful for methodologies that measure differences in domain free list content and length as well as relational organization of items within domains by analysis of interview tasks such as free lists, pile sorts, triadic comparisons, frame substitutions sets, rankings, ratings and paired comparisons (Bernard 1995, Boster 1986 and 1994, Borgatti 1996). In general, experts will know more about an area of knowledge and be able to manipulate or talk about those bits of knowledge. For example, a botanical expert will know many more types of plants and be able to name, describe, identify, and organize information about those plants than someone who is not an expert in botany.

If a researcher has experts and nonexperts complete the same interview tasks, experts will usually supply much more knowledge in greater detail than nonexperts. But, nonexperts may provide the information in a much different way that is still important to the bulk of the population of a cultural group, since there are far more nonexperts than experts in most populations. The analysis of data comparing experts and nonexperts is used to describe the **intracultural variation** in cognitive knowledge, beliefs, and structuring for a particular domain. Usually, the required characteristics for classification of consultants as either experts and nonexperts are defined in literature review or exploratory fieldwork prior to either the experimental fieldwork or interview analysis. If a researcher is uncertain of how to identify experts, there are methods for identifying experts and nonexperts within a sample population when they are unknown, either by the particle model or the wave model of knowledge. This is one of the goals of Cultural consensus modeling, which evaluates the expertise of consultants by how many "particles" or "items" of knowledge they list as well as how well they agree with the rest of the sample group (Romney et al. 1986, 1987, D'Andrade 1987). Alternately, the "wave" approach to identifying experts vs. nonexperts evaluates not only how many pieces of knowledge consultants have, but more importantly, how *deep* their knowledge of the domain is in terms of functional ability, personal utilization, and classification ability.

In this experimental study, most of my consultants were experts at reenacting, though many were considered much more "expert" than others by both their own evaluation and by their peers.

Research Populations and Environment

Every detail is important on reproduction garments. Period-authentic laces, ties, and toggles are used.

Consultants, in general, were located by the snowball technique. The snowball technique was described by Boster (1994), and is a simple but effective method of locating consultants by having consultants recommend others who would be good candidates for interview. Finding the initial consultants in each sample group, however, required other methods. The technique for finding consultants within each sample grouping is described below with the definitions for grouping terms. Demographic variables such as age, gender, ethnicity, and context were recorded for analysis, but because the snowball technique is not random, there were no preset goals of obtaining set numbers of these sociodemographic categories. I did have minimum quotas for several of the groupings, a minimum of 5 experts each in Native American, Traditional Chinese medicine, European traditional, and Modern/Ecclectic herbalism and a minimum of 15 nonexperts in herbal medicine. Then, 3 experts each in civil war, S.C.A. and RenFaire reenacting.

Because the original goal of my fieldwork as to research herbal remedy use, many of my consultants were chosen or recommended because of their knowledge of herbal remedies. As I searched for more information on reenactment culture in general instead of herbal remedies in particular, I interviewed other reenactors without regard to their knowledge on herbs. The only interviews included in this data are from reenactors, many of whom used herbal remedies. The first salient term is the identification of a person eligible for interview. Because I am interested in reenactors from an emic point of view, I only interviewed individuals who stated that they participated in reenacting.

To identify individuals for interview, I relied on a variety of simple techniques. Often I initiated conversation about an individual's garb, artifacts, or merchandise to establish preliminary rapport and evaluate the individual's knowledge of herbal remedies (or later, reenacting). Once this was done, and the individuals were at ease, I simply asked "Can you recommend anyone who is an expert in herbs?", or "Do you know anyone who could tell me more about reenacting?" Employees at alternative bookstores; people in small shops or merchant stalls with displays of locally produced herbal products, historical-period supplies (one knitting/and wool supply vendor was particularly helpful); and a variety of other merchants were very fruitful areas to gather information. In addition to finding individuals to formally interview, many of these informal encounters filled my notebooks with data about the habits, customs, and material culture of reenactors. Additional consultants were obtained by simply asking people around the University of Missouri campus if they would be interested in completing a short interview. In the campus setting, many individuals are quite willing to participate in interview projects, whether they are students, faculty, or staff.

Interview Environment

Interviews were conducted in either private, semi-private, or public settings at the preference of the consultant. We sought a location that was comfortable to the consultant, such as their office, tent, home, or a neutral location such as a coffee shop. Both the consultant and I sat and faced each other during the interviews.

Interview schedules were used to guide interviews and ensure that all questions were answered. Potential consultants were allowed to see a summary of the interview structure and questions to determine whether they felt comfortable with the interview process and subject matter. Once consultants agreed to the interview, a time for the interview was scheduled. While some consultants scheduled a later appointment for the interview, many immediately began the interview. At the beginning of the actual interview, consultants were given an informed consent form approved by the University of Missouri Internal Research Board Human Subjects Committee. This form contained contact information for the university, the MU Anthropology Department, my advisor, and myself. Consultants were also given a business card with my contact information. To complete this book, some consultants were recontacted and asked follow-up questions. Only informants who had indicated at the time of their interview that they wished to be contacted at a future date were recontacted.

Interview Tools

Interview information was recorded with pencil and paper onto empty data recording sheets or onto a small reporter's-style notepad. When permission was given by the consultant, the interviews were recorded on an audio tape in a micro cassette recorder. Interview information from these forms and tapes was recorded directly into Excel spreadsheets.

If the consultant consented, a camera loaded with 35 mm slide film and/or standard photographic film was used to take photographs of the interview settings as well as artifacts the consultants used or constructed. During or after the interview, consultants frequently wished to show me favorite artifacts.

Interview Experiences

Individual differences existed among the consultants, often typical of a particular subgroup. For instance, I conducted several interviews with Native American herbal practitioners which were quite different from the other interviews in my research. I had to adapt my training and methodology to perform the interviews in a way deemed culturally appropriate by members of the society. Before obtaining permission to perform an interview, I had to meet and converse with several individuals. These individuals 1) made recommendations to elders or practitioners about whether or not I should be seen, 2) provided helpful information for appropriate behavior, 3) evaluated my sincerity and willingness to listen, and 4) chose to whether or not reveal themselves as practitioners or not during an initial conversation phase of the interviews. In many cases, particularly at PowWows or scheduled interviews, several other individuals were present or "dropped by". These individuals were a part of the evaluation process and often turned out to be practitioners themselves who were evaluating me incognito or their intermediaries. If the contact stated that they were not interested, I respected their wishes and did not pursue them further.

Four out of the five Native American practitioners I formally interviewed refused a tape recorder during the interview. Instead, I was required to demonstrate respect by conducting the interview in a traditional method. I was asked questions to determine my seriousness and background. Then I listened to the practitioner, asking the questions as prompts when it was requested or letting them select the question order. I could write down information, but performed appropriately by reciting the information back to them to demonstrate my understanding in a traditional learning method. If my repetition was incorrect, the practitioner corrected me and explained again to clarify. Personally, I found this to be a wonderful way of conducting interviews. Though I was initially flustered, since this is quite different from the training I received in methods classes and the literature, I rapidly adapted with the patience of my consultants. My own Native American heritage was an important factor in these interactions, as my face and features were scrutinized, and I was asked to provide information about my ancestry as my consultants searched for a common connection between us. That tenuous connection was often used by my consultants as a basis for rapport and recognizing me as distant kin who needed instruction in Native traditions.

The advantages of the format preferred by the Native American practitioners are many. The consultant has a comfortable role as teacher in the format with which they are familiar. In addition, both parties are able to ensure that ideas were clearly conveyed. These interviews were very satisfying for both parties and ensured that consultants did not feel like "test subjects" or "experimental objects/animals". I became the student, in many cases quite literally sitting on the ground at my consultant's knee to receive instruction from an elder.

Four of my European herbal practitioners rarely had the opportunity to perform professionally outside of their paracultural communities in the Society of Creative Anachronism or Renaissance Faires. They were quite friendly and willing to be interviewed, but not all potential practitioners were able to dedicate the time needed to conduct a full interview. Because they were uncomfortable performing outside their communities, these consultants were interviewed in either S.C.A. or Renaissance Faire settings and in their period persona.

The consultants were a little nervous about their performances, but comfortable and very willing to answer questions, often asking "Is there anything else I could tell you?" and encouraging their friends to "come and try it". This worked particularly well in the setting of the Society of Creative Anachronism events and Wiccan covens. Both sub-cultural groups value information and learning, and were quite eager to quiz *me* afterwards in order to obtain more information sources.

Fieldwork Interaction with Sampled Populations

While interviews serve to collect data from consultants, less formal interaction with sampled populations is necessary to establish rapport. Participant observation is the ideal way to truly understand the emic perspective of the population you are studying, but true participant observation is not always possible. Less intense interactions with consultants include informal conversations, observation of activities, and establishment of friendship with key consultants. The question then becomes "Exactly how does one locate and establish contact with key consultants?" This question is particularly salient in research settings in the United States. While one could act like a news reporter from the evening news and stand about with a camera and notepad waiting for consultants to pass by, this is not the best way to obtain targeted sample groups. It is also not the best way to achieve the interactions necessary to establish rapport.

As discussed above, the first method I used was to frequent contexts which consultants were expected to frequent. These included providers/merchants who sold herbs and herbal remedies; supplies for period reproductions; and event merchants as well as cultural events where reenactors were gathered for living history demonstrations. Before I attempted to gain permission to conduct interview, I observed and interacted with reenactors in an informal way to learn more about typical activities and accepted behaviors. During this time, I talked informally with individuals, asking questions and generally becoming familiar with the environment. After identifying and establishing rapport with initial consultants, I

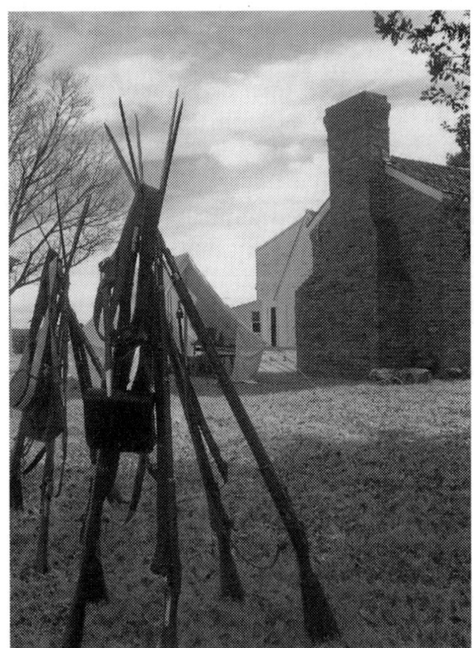

Every attempt is made to recreate the period feel or bed through use of ortifacts and historic settings. Muskets and gear arranged in a Union camp.

Photo by Steve Shore.

was able to begin asking for interviews. I also observed and conversed with reenactors at PowWows, Society for Creative Anachronism events, Renaissance Faires, a Rendezvous event, living history demonstrations, and Civil War reenactments.

I was able to conduct participant observation at S.C.A. events and Renaissance Faires. With the assistance of a few key informants, I was able to achieve the immersion which typifies participant observation and that allowed me to participate in activities alongside my sample population as "one of them" at Society of Creative Anachronism events. Unlike a place of business or an event designed to demonstrate to an audience, these events stress the need for everyone to "remain period" by dressing, speaking, and behaving in the agreed-upon form of "the modern middle ages." The boundary line between the performers and audience is not present, since everyone is participating in the same activity—group play. Since these events exist in a discrete time period and location, the researcher can "go there" and stay in the participant observation mode for a prolonged period of up to 10 days. This was a valuable way to establish rapport that is much more like standard anthropological fieldwork methods than other contexts. During participant observation, I attended community activities and helped with tasks like food preparation, "riding the tents" during a thunderstorm, and dying cloth. I also attended ritual performances like "court"and "battles" as well as the classes on medieval and S.C.A.-related topics that are at the core of this re-enactment-oriented community. My participant observation experiences are discussed more in the sections on the S.C.A. and Renaissance Faires in the next section of the book.

Conclusions

In summary, I located and established rapport with members of my sample populations in a variety of context-specific ways. I was able to conduct participant observation with the S.C.A. group and interactions that included conversation, observation, and interviews with the other sample populations. The practice establishing rapport with the S.C.A. population had the added benefit of making it easier to establish rapport with individuals in the similar, if more demonstration-oriented atmosphere of the Renaissance Faires, Civil War and other living history reenactments, and Pow-Wows.

Name ______________________________ Date ____________________

Assignments

Why is it important to consider the difference between the terms *informant* and *consultant*? Which would you rather be called?

Why is *subject* not appropriate for the people anthropologists study?

What is the difference between an *expert* and a *nonexpert*?

Give an example of an expert and the criteria for deciding that person is an expert.

What is a domain?

Give an example of a domain and the items that would be placed inside it.

Name of Domain: **Items in this domain include. . . .**	
1	
2	
3	
4	
5	
6	
7	
8	
9	
10	

Design a Free List Exercise

Now, think of another domain. For this domain, think of one where you know both an expert and a nonexpert. For example, you may choose a topic from one of your classes, where you could ask your professor to be the expert and a fellow student to be the non-expert. You might use one of your parents or boss as an expert. Ask the nonexpert list items in this domain on one form. Then, ask the expert to list items. Compare the two lists. Who listed more items? How did the expert act while listing compared to the non-expert? What does this experience tell you about nonexperts and experts?

For more advanced practice, you could have the expert and nonexpert do one or more of the following with the items in the domain:

For the items listed, please:

- rank them in order of most important to least important

Name ______________________________ Date ____________________

- tell me which of the items is the most typical, or representative example of a __________ (insert name of the domain)?
- mark which ones you "like", "dislike", or are neutral about

You could also have your consultants sort the items into piles and tell you the names of the piles (pile sorting).

How else could you use the data from your lists? Describe at least 3 ways.

Name of Domain **Items in this domain include. . . . .**		**Nonexpert's list** **(** **)**

Name of Domain **Items in this domain include. . . . .**		**Expert's list** **(** **)**

Fieldwork Methods and Tools

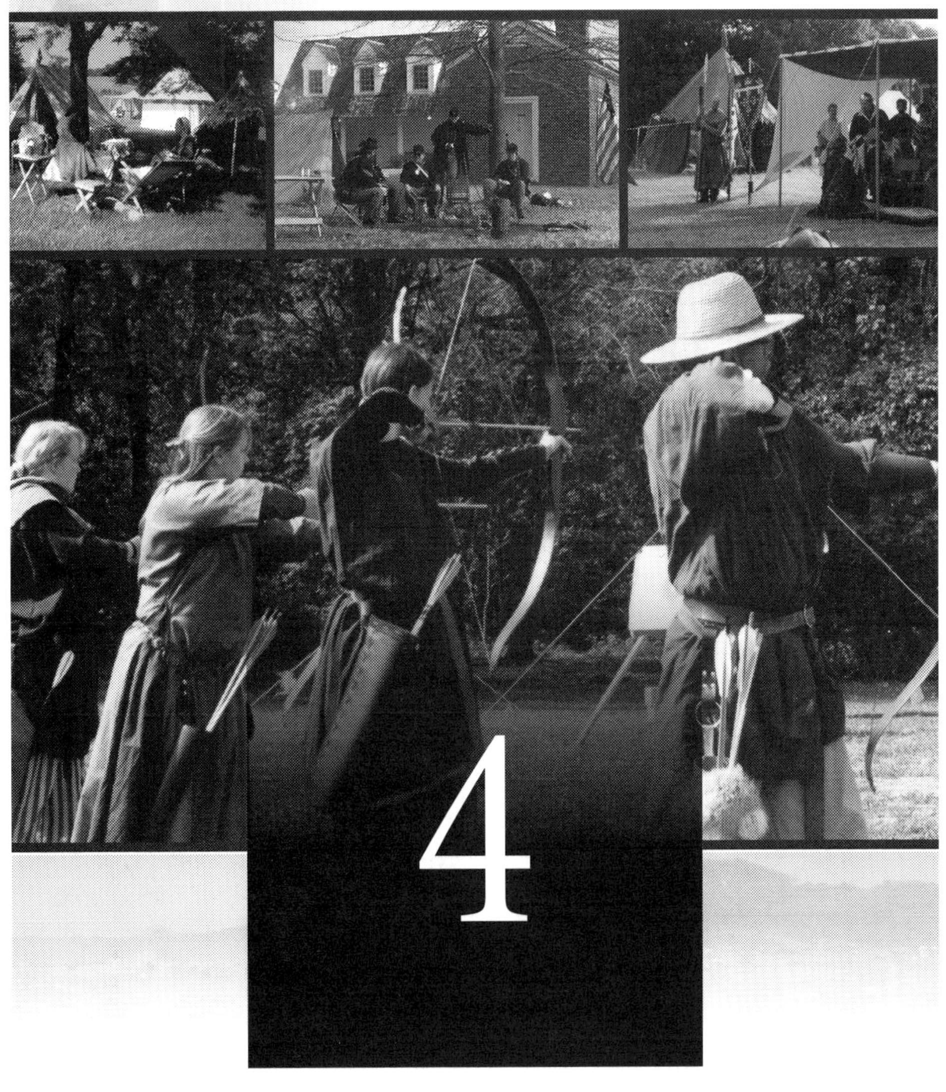

4

Introduction

In an anthropological project, one of the most important procedures is research design. The methodological approach utilized in fieldwork and analysis shapes what cultural units are gathered as data. The format in which these units of data are gathered, in turn, circumscribes the scope of available analysis methods. Available analysis methods then determine what results the researcher can present and the interpretive power of the entire project. At every step, choice of method shapes the structure of the data gathered and its ultimate usefulness in understanding the anthropological phenomenon being investigated.

It is important, then, to choose the sampling techniques that are the best suited to answering the goals and questions of the project. Even more important is the precaution of ensuring that you, as the researcher, are actually gathering the appropriate units of data to actually answer your questions. Failure to gather the appropriate units results in a project with data that doesn't apply to your research questions and much frustration as you search for a way to "get at" the answers to your questions. For most research questions, however, a variety of techniques can successfully gather similar forms of the same units of data, giving you some freedom to choose among methods. It is important to consider more than your own convenience as a researcher when choosing, though. Some techniques of data collection provide the bits of data in more desirable formats for the researcher, but they may be unpalatable (i.e. *boring*) to the consultants performing the task. The final methodology, then, must be a reasonable compromise between the researcher's desire for explicit, complete information in an easily-processed format and the consultants' patience for often tedious tasks.

This chapter describes several methods of gathering and analyzing data that can be used in a variety of settings. Once you master these basic skills, you can choose to apply them in topics of interest to you. At the end of this chapter are several small exercises which will give you practice with these new skills.

Basic Ethnographic Methods

Ethnography is a holistic, recorded description of a culture, subculture, or paraculture. Classically, an ethnography has been a *written* account, but the availability of visual and audio media has resulted in a growing number of multimedia ethnographies now that integrate sound and images. Doing ethnography is the process of collecting the information, or data, which will be used to describe and represent the people of a culture. A variety of methods are used in ethnography.

Much information about the culture being studied can be gathered from literature and document review. Many would be ethnographers begin by trying to discover what, if anything, has already been recorded about the group or phenomena they wish to study. This preliminary background research can be quite invaluable. Imagine traveling to a remote location and setting up camp with a people, struggling to learn their language enough to even greet them properly, and spending a year in the field with them..... only to come back and discover that a complete dictionary of their language was available in your university library! Background research lets the researcher discover what has already been done and make more informed and considered decisions about their research topic and questions. These research questions shape the rest of the project, determining who and where will be studied and what data needs to be collected. In the course of fieldwork, research questions are often refined and revised as new data is incorporated into the researcher's model, but the initial research questions are necessary for scientific inquiry.

Observation

Once a culture and preliminary research questions are selected, the first and most basic method in ethnographic fieldwork is to observe the culture in question. In the past, observation was a spectator sport, with outsiders recording the behaviors and characteristics of the people being observed much as ethologists did with animal behavior studies. This is called the ***etic***, or outsider's approach. The hallmark method of anthropological ethnography, however, is ***participant observation***. In participant observation, the ethnographer participates in the activities being studied. By doing what the people being observed do, the ethnographer learns what it is like from the ***emic***, or insider's perspective. It also greatly aids in establishing rapport, a feeling of closeness and empathy. The people are better able to relate to the ethnographer and can interact comfortably with the participant observer, often under the guise of helping them learn how to perform various activities properly. The ethnographer becomes much like a child being enculturated into the society, and members of the society are more at ease if they know where the ethnographer fits into the scheme of things. This can also be beneficial for the ethnographer in other ways. In this childlike learning role, mistakes that are offensive in adults are often laughed away as the mistakes of a child and unintentional gaffs are treated with tolerance and gently corrected. Often, key informants or elders in the society will take the ethnographer under their wing as a fictive child, providing them with a place in the society, much-appreciated social support, and entrée into aspects of cultural life that are not usually accessible to true outsiders. This closeness and incorporation into the society helps the ethnographer to enculturate and better understand the emic perspective.

Descriptions of the culture include lists of the artifacts and behaviors observed. It is common to inventory the items for sale at different vendors, descriptions of homes, clothing, makeup, hairstyles, foods, currency, calendars, and customs. Often, photographs or video are recorded. Sample artifacts may be collected or purchased as examples.

Interviews

In the course of participant observation, the ethnographer collects data in many informal or loosely structured ways. Conversations overheard, casual commentary, and observations are all important sources of information. Informal interviews are conversations that the ethnographer has with consultants without a prestructured set of questions. A formal interview includes a preset list of questions to be asked by the ethnographer. The questions in the formal interview may be ***structured*** or ***unstruc-***

tured, and the type of information requested may be either ***qualitative*** or ***quantitative***. Most interviews include a little of each type of questions and data. Structured questions are those that require a bounded, or limited range for the answer. Survey questions and multiple choice exam questions are good examples of structured questions. In a multiple choice exam question, there are usually two -five choices for the person to choose among. An unstructured question is more like a short answer or essay question. The respondent is expected to answer in their own words or phrases. Either of these can be quantitative, that is, an answer that expresses a discrete quantity, or number. A qualitative question is not a discrete quantity. Instead, it is an answer that provides a quality (blue, good, cold, sad, hate, etc . . .).

All of these have their place in describing a culture, and most ethnographies contain both qualitative and quantitative data. Over the course of an ethnography, a researcher usually uses both quantitative and qualitative questions. Qualitative unstructured questions are usually used for gathering exploratory data and learning enough background to prepare more informed structured questions. Ethnographers often collect life histories, personal narratives, and the answers to open-ended questions like "tell me about. . . ." or "why do people believe/do. . . ."

A summary or report of the information collected through these sorts of interviews are interpreted and presented by the ethnographer. Often, quotes from specific individuals are presented as representative of cultural beliefs. Analysis methods called **text analysis** are used to identify common **themes** or motifs and present them in a more systematic way than simply printing the complete text of all of the interviews. Themes often indicate the presence of cultural domains that the ethnographer studies in more detail.

Cultural Domains

A basic way to begin an ethnographic description and understanding of a group is to learn items of cultural knowledge like their special terms, artifacts, and customs. Collecting lists of the items in a cultural ***domain***, or cognitive subject category, from several consultants lets a researcher describe the items included within those domains as well as variation among differing subgroups of my sampled consultants. For this to work, comparable bits of data, or units, are needed within each domain. There are several techniques for collecting systematic, comparable data on cultural domains. The most common techniques include free listing, pile sorting, triads, paired comparisons, and frame substitutions. I begin by discussing how the techniques relate to each other, then describe the characteristics and methods of free listing, pile sorting, and frame substitution.

Collecting Data on Cultural Domains

The purpose of research design is to determine which of the available methods best gather the data necessary to fulfill one's research goals. The function, then, of research methods, or techniques, is to gather *pertinent*, or **salient** data—the information that can be used to answer your research questions and test your hypotheses. Several standard techniques are available to gather such data. The techniques described here include: (1) For eliciting lists of the items that belong in a domain: various types of free listing, and (2) for understanding how items within domains relate to each other and are organized: pile sorting, triads, paired comparisons, and frame substitutions. In addition, approaches that have been found useful for studying intracultural variation within domains are discussed, including cultural consensus analysis, qualitative text analysis, and quantitative text analysis. The first step, and the one that forms the foundation of the descriptive process, is to elicit the items within the domains being investigated.

Methodological Approaches to Sampling Cultural Domains

1. Free Listing

Free listing stands alone as a first step technique. Free list data can be used for many tasks where consultants are asked to manipulate or arrange a set if items. Free listing is used to gather the names of the items within a domain. The members of a domain are things that belong together in a group. Unlike the other methods, free listing does not give relational data of how the items in the list are organized, but additional steps can be added to listing to do this.

Free listing as a technique is easy and inexpensive to construct. You simply ask consultants to fill the domain for you by listing all of the kinds of ____. Free listing is easy to administer because the consultants can easily understand what information is requested of them and comply (Figure 4.1). You ask several people, expert and nonexpert, to free list items in the same domain and then compare and compile their lists. It has the advantage of letting you elicit the membership of items (plants, foods, traits, weapons, tools, terms, holidays, etc . . .) in a domain. Several simple techniques can help you evaluate the ***saliency*** (relative importance) of items in the domain via frequency, rank order, and paired associations. When you combine the lists of several people, many items will be listed by several (sometimes all) of the consultants while others are listed by only a few or one. The frequency of each item is an indicator of its salience, as is its relative rank on the lists. For example, if you have students free list types of blue jeans, "Levi's" may not be the first type of jeans listed by each student, but it will be on the most of the students' lists. Levi's jeans are highly salient. They would be even more salient if they *were* the first or second type of jeans listed as well. A brand of jeans listed by only one or two students and appeared very low on the list of those students would not be as salient.

As you can see, salience is relative and used to compare items within the same domain. The sample used is an important determinant in the items gathered by free listing, so a careful researcher should be careful to sample people who are representative of the cultural group in question and to also sample enough people. It often surprises beginning researchers that an adequate sample size for free listing does not need to be very large. Twenty to thirty individuals can be sufficient, especially if several experts are included. As few as four or five experts may give an exhaustive list, though this smaller sample will not have the same salience scores as lists collected from "average" members of the population because experts know so many items and tend to think of them

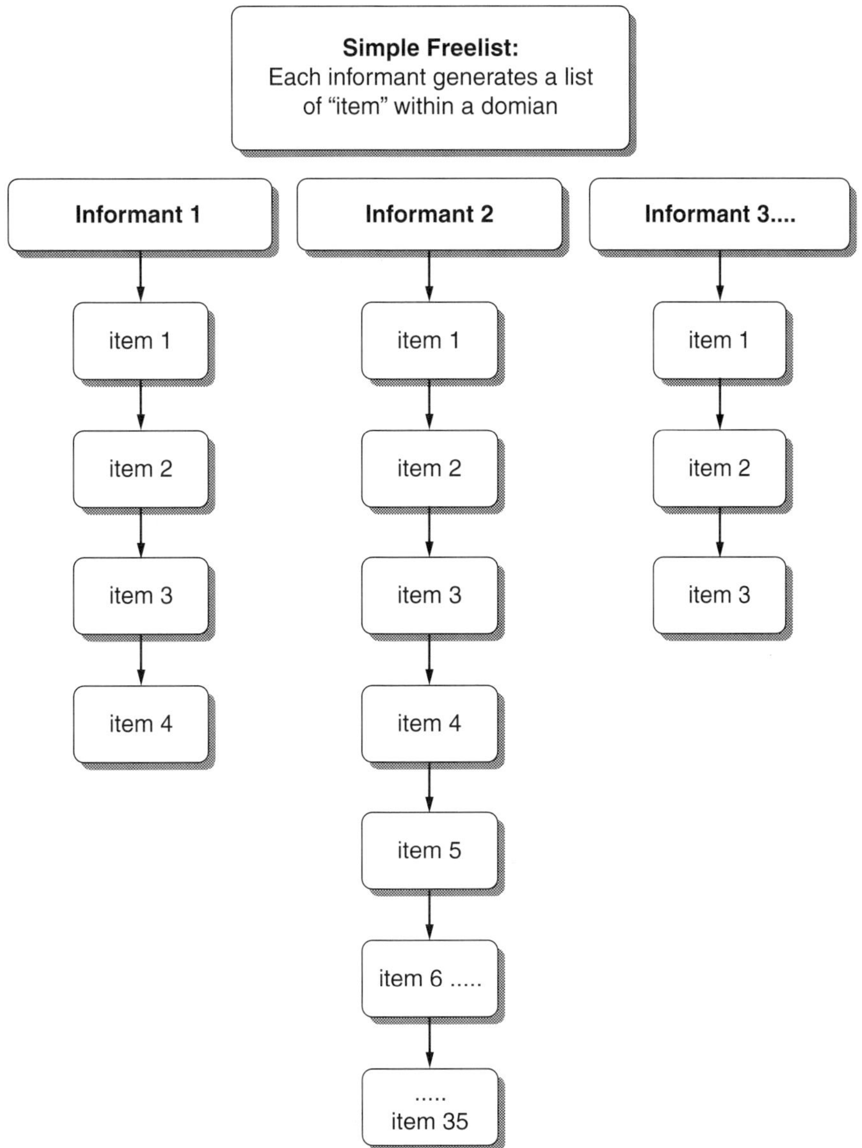

Figure 4.1

differently than nonexperts in a field. After the lists start to become redundant, containing the same items with few or no new items discovered, the free list sample is usually considered large enough. This often happens at around thirty individuals.

Free listing is often the very useful "first step" in further exploration of a domain. Although free listing does not tell you how the members of a domain are cognitively arranged, it does let you construct the tools that will allow you to discover that information. The data from a free list can be used to construct tasks like pile sorts, triads, frame substitutions (using both items and traits of those items), paired comparisons, and numerous types of survey questions. In addition, free lists can reveal important or unique items that warrant further investigation through either structured tasks like those listed above or open-ended questions.

Other Types of Free Lists

A variation on the free list method is successive free listing, described by Gery Ryan (Ryan et al. 1999). Successive free builds upon an initial or primary simple free list to reveal further information about each item on that initial free list (Figure 4.2). After having a consultant generate a free list, the interviewer then goes back and asks another free list

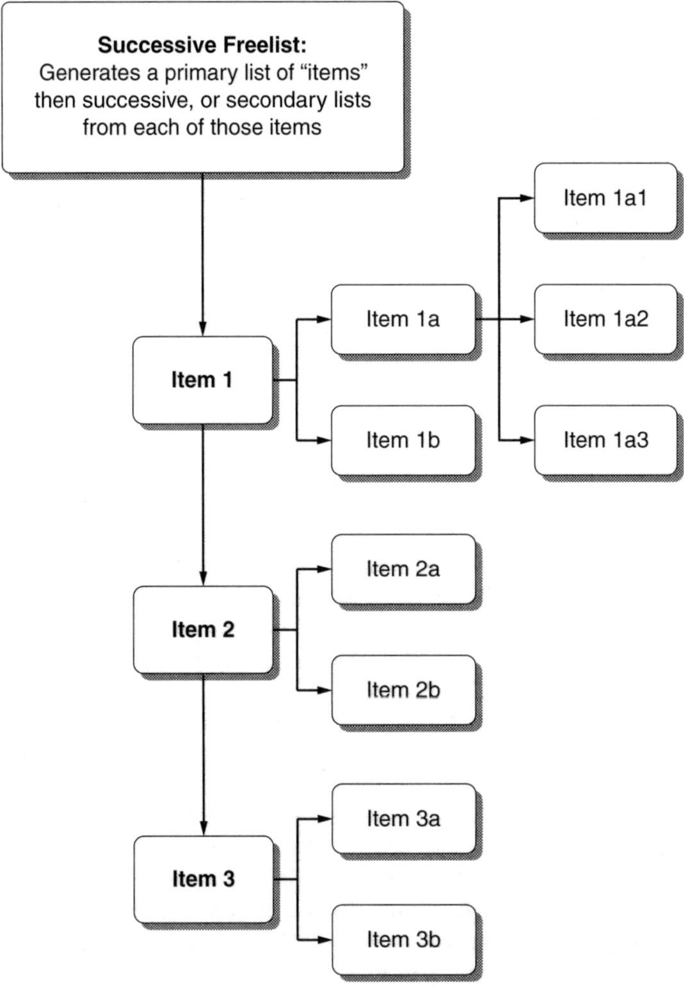

Figure 4.2

question of each of the items from the primary free list. The next step is attaching another, successive, free list to each of the items on the secondary list. The successive free list method branches away from the primary free list in an ever-branching, treelike network.

Another variation on a simple free list is to return to the items in a primary free list in a non-successive way. In this method, which I refer to as spoked free listing, you begin by having consultants generate a free list. For each of the items on that primary free list, a series of questions is asked. While the questions may be secondary free lists as in successive free listing, they may also include ratings or yes/no questions. For instance, after students listed types of blue jeans above, they could be asked to go back and rate whether each type of blue jean was "cool" or "geeky", "cheap" or "classy", to simply rate them on some scale of 1–10, or even to rank the items in their own list by various criteria. Alternatively, behaviors could be studied by asking the students to mark how often or whether they wear that type of jeans. Perceptions about social standing and customs could be gathered by asking students a judgmental question like "what type of people wear x type of jeans?" It is easy to see how a simple list could be used to gather much useful and interesting information about a domain.

For a spoked free list, each question in the series, however, returns to the item from the primary list (Figure 4.3). The most useful function of this method is that it allows the researcher to ask different categorization questions about the primary free list

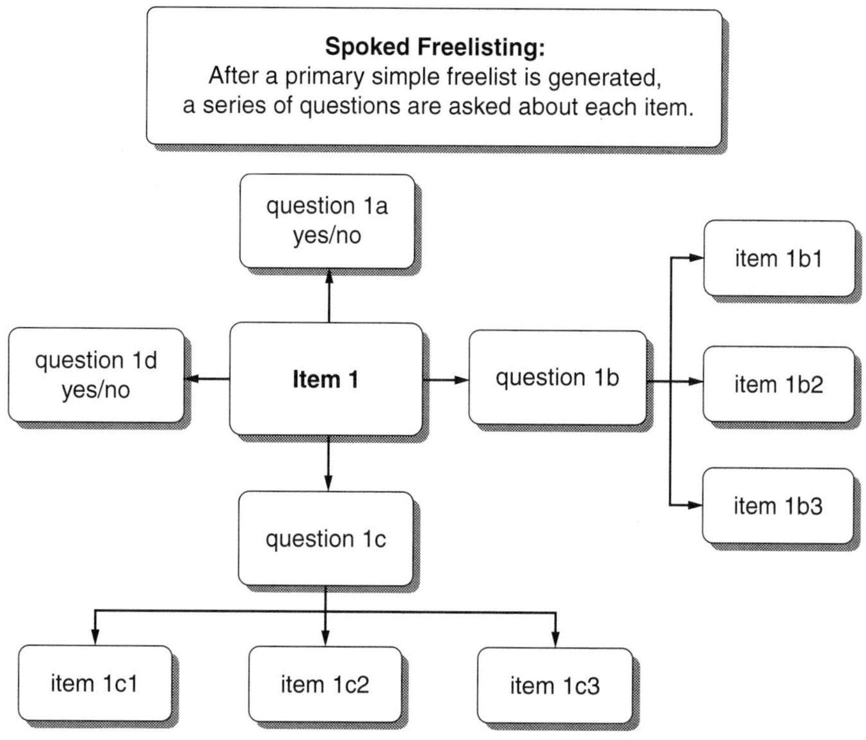

Figure 4.3

items. This allows a better understanding of domains where the items have multiple subdomains or belong to multiple groupings.

2. Gathering Relational Data

Pile sorting, triads, paired comparisons, and frame substitutions are techniques designed to reveal relational data on the items within a domain. In short, they are used to discover how people think about things in a domain or arrange/organize the information in their minds. Each is suited to different particular situations or questions, and has subtle differences. In general, you use them to discover how individuals perceptually arrange, group, or relate items. You can also determine what the important characteristics are for group membership. The data gathered allows a researcher to discover the classification system people use for that domain. Pile sorting is the most commonly used of the tasks designed to reveal relational data.

In pile sorting, consultants are simply asked to arrange items or representations of items in either a constrained (you tell them how many piles to make) or an unconstrained manner. You can either use real items such as birds, insects, bottles, etc . . ., or slips of paper with representations of items in the form of words, photos, or illustrations. The important detail in this technique is to remember to only place one thing or concept per card. Unlike the other techniques, you have the choice of having the consultant do a single pile sort or successive pile sorts. You can allow the consultant to 1) arrange the items in alternate patterns at the same level or 2) arrange each successive pile into further subdivided piles to obtain a hierarchical taxonomy. After the consultant sorts the items into piles, you record the items in each pile and ask the consultant to tell you the name of each pile and the criteria used to include or exclude things from each pile. A pile sort can be combined with a rating or ranking task. Rating tasks have consultants rate each item on a scale (usually of most to least) while ranking tasks have the consultants rank items within each pile.

Frame substitutions, also called sentence frames or frame elicitation, produce yes/no or true/false data. Their name comes from the fact that they are structured as the frames of sentences like "can _x_ come from _y_?" or "treatment _*x*_ is a good treatment for illness _y._" The ethnographer inserts items from two lists—a list of *x*'s and a list of y's—gathered from free lists. By asking a series of these questions for all of your terms, you can measure differences between individual culture and shared culture. Compared to the other methods, they are especially suited to determining causative relationships and as such are a welcome resolution to the vagueness of meaning provided by statistical correlations. With a frame substitution, you can explicitly ask consultants how items are related. Frame substitutions are appropriate for smaller lists than the pile sorts, but differ in that you compare two classes of items (2 lists) to each other pairwise. Though frame substitutions gather a lot of precise data, they can be repetitive and tedious for consultants if you ask them to complete too many.

Pile sorts are best for gathering relational data about domains with lots of items because they do not feel as repetitive or tedious to consultants. It is generally believed that consultants like pile sorting and rarely consider it boring (Borgatti 1999, Boster

1994). Asking why piles go together, what they are, and combining other techniques like ranking and rating can reveal wealth of information. Though it does not yield the same quantitative data as other relational techniques, the richness of the qualitative data and the wealth of information keep pile sorting a popular and very useful option. Problems with pile sorting can occur with the natural tendency of some people to be lumpers or splitters. This problem occurs in free (unconstrained) pile sorts. You can address this by choosing constrained pile sorts. A constrained pile sort is where you specify how many piles a consultant can have, preventing them from trying to place everything in one or two piles (lumpers) or each item in it's own pile (splitters.) A lot of the variation in pile sorting can also be due to the nature of your stimulus. Photos, actual objects, and other representations of domain items can cause on-the-spot categorization based upon traits or form of the stimulus, not cultural beliefs about the items. Stephen Borgatti (1999) recommends being as abstract as possible if you want to elicit cultural beliefs, not sorting ability.

Frame substitutions usually require computer software for analysis. An old but standard program called ANTHROPAC is often used. The ANTHROPAC yes/no x times y matrix is the easiest way to perform this analysis. There are many good ethnographic software programs available now, and the adventurous researcher can even write their own formulae for numerous other statistical software packages. In ANTHROPAC, simply adding several matrices (1 per consultant) allows you to get multidimensional scaling. Very good for particular types of data, especially causative factors in medical anthropology, frame substitutions were used in classic anthropological studies by L. Garro (1986), who measured folk medical knowledge, by J. Boster (1986) in distinguishing manioc cultivars among the Aguaruna, and Chavez et al. (1995) in their exploration of cancer risk factors. The individual questions, presented one at a time, are fairly quick and easy for consultants, but they become tedious and boring. For just 25 animals and 25 attributes, or descriptors, you have 25 x 25 = 625 questions! If you want to include frame substitutions in your research design, you must be sure the domains, items, attributes, etc . . . are culturally relevant, small, and make sense or the consultants won't tolerate the questions and will become biased due to fatigue.

Useful Approaches for Studying Intracultural Variation

There are a variety of approaches for thinking about intracultural variation within domains. Important and widely used approaches for studying knowledge in anthropology include Cultural Consensus Analysis, conceptualizing knowledge and intracultural variation as a combination of particle and wave models, the simple wave model of knowledge, and a combination of qualitative text analysis and quantitative text analysis. In particular, researchers choose among these approaches because of the different ways they identify experts and nonexperts. If you want to learn more, references to important scholars in these areas are listed at the end of the chapter.

1. Cultural Consensus

An important construct in cultural anthropology, intracultural variation is closely associated with the concepts of experts, nonexperts, and cultural consensus modeling. Each of these terms is defined and explained in terms of the structure and content of cultural domains. Intracultural variation is simply the variation that exists among the individuals within a culture (Bernard 1995). Variation within culture can occur along several lines. Some variation among individuals is to be expected, since a single individual does not hold the sum total of a culture's contents. Knowledge can be distributed among individuals as a part of their individual attributes. Variation also occurs between subgroups within a culture, wherein members of the same group have more overlap or consensus in their knowledge than members of larger cultural groupings.

A standard way of measuring and revealing intracultural variation is analysis of the differences in free list content and length. Cognitive differences have been measured by comparing relational organization with triads, pile sorts, frame substitution tests, rankings, ratings, and paired comparisons. Cultural consensus modeling, described by Romney et al. (1986, 1987) is a method for determining "cultural knowledge" that attempts to quantitatively demonstrate 1) an estimate of cultural competence, or knowledge level, for each consultant and 2) how to infer "correct" answers. Cultural consensus modeling attempts to meet these two goals on the basis of the belief that knowledge can be inferred from consensus among a sample of people. According to this model, consultants who are more competent (more expert) will have higher consensus and more culturally "correct" answers in their domain of expertise. In order for Consensus Analysis to be valid, it is assumed that for a domain:

1. There is a common truth, or fixed answer in shared cultural reality.
2. There is local independence, and consultant-item responses are random variables that satisfy conditional independence (conditional on the correct answer key.)
3. Items are homogenous, so all questions have the same difficulty level for all consultants

Analysis with cultural consensus modeling creates measures of cultural competence (variables symbolized by "D's") that allow the researcher to compare the competence of the consultants. Since these estimates are comparable to other groups' or cultures' measures, one can compare among groups as well as within groups.

Consensus analysis also allows the identification of experts and nonexperts, or novices, in particular domains by the differences in their free list length (# items displayed in domain.) Experts are expected to have more items in their domain of expertise, and to be able to name both the highly salient (for the entire group) items and a number of unique items not known to novices. Nonexperts, by contrast, are those with smaller domains centered on a few core items that are typically either highly salient to them or highly ubiquitous in their society.

In relational exercises like pile sorts, triads, and paired comparisons, experts are expected to have greater consistency as well as greater sophistication in organization than novices. This sophistication, or "expertise", is based upon the assumptions of cultural consensus modeling. In consensus modeling, if there is a "correct" answer, then experts are those with more consistently correct answers according to the sample group's most common answers. Weller (1984) used four measures of consensus under the cultural consensus model to identify experts: 1) reliability, 2) overall consensus, 3) degree of consensus, and 4) index of competency. All four of these measures are based upon the assumptions that consensus is "correct", and that the most culturally competent consultants are those that agree the most with the other individuals in the sample group.

The problem with this is that many types of knowledge are not democratic. For example, most people in 15th century Europe believed that the Earth was flat. Did this make it true? Experts have much more training in their area of expertise than nonexperts. Take, for instance, an exam in your chemistry or genetics class. If most of the class answered question #3 as answer B, does this make it correct even though correct answer is A according to the knowledge held by the professor and textbook? According to the Cultural Consensus Model, the most average person is the most expert. This is very useful for finding information for marketing or language research, but not for technical information. Think carefully about your research questions and the type of research you are conducting when you choose an approach to understanding intracultural variation and determining expertise.

2. Alternatives to the Cultural Consensus Model

Of course, there is another way that experts and novices are identified in research. Outside of consensus modeling, experts are often labeled by their roles. Physicians, medicine men, and other health care practitioners, for example, are expected to be experts in medicine. Ph.D.s in botany and zoology are expected to be experts in plant and animal domains, respectively. Experts are not necessarily people who agree the most with everyone. Instead, experts are individuals with a great deal of training and/or experience in a domain. People without any apparent special training or exposure to the finer details of a particular domain are assumed to be nonexperts since they are not expected to have any pragmatic reason for expertise.

Experts may also be identified by the snowball technique. For example, in my herbal medicine research, I located few initial experts via their professions on the assumption that licensed practitioners would be experts. In exploratory, informal conversations and interviews, I asked these initial experts to recommend other experts for my sample group. In addition, members of a subculture can be asked to identify the acknowledged experts in their group. As another example, I asked members of the populations I sampled from who they considered to be experts and who they used or recommended as herbal practitioners. Searching within likely contexts such as subcultures, venues, or environments experts are likely to frequent allows a narrower search for potential consultants.

Jim Boster's (1987) used an approach to intracultural variation that is more balanced. He agrees with proponents of the Cultural Consensus Model that by understanding how individuals learn, remember and transmit cultural knowledge you can understand how cultures work. He also believes that you should study how individuals vary to build models of how collective understandings emerge from individual learning. Within this field, though, there is a disagreement over what the patterning of intracultural variation. Intracultural variation is the pattern of disagreement among members of a community across a variety of domains.

There are two theories, or models, of how consultant knowledge can be described. Boster calls these two models particle theory and wave theory. The particle theory holds that knowledge is coherent, in discrete pieces actively constructed into models that add up in more knowledgeable people. Learning in particle theory, would be individual. The wave theory proposes that different individuals have different pieces of the picture, passively acquired, and sets of rules about knowledge that allow them to deal with novel situations. People would learn from the social or physical environment. The cultural consensus model is therefore a particle theory of knowledge.

D'Andrade (1987), by contrast, proposes the wave theory of knowledge. For example, D'Andrade used word association tests, which have no single correct answer. He found that subjects choosing modal word association responses had higher IQs, better education, and were more reliably knowledgeable. Expertise is based upon an individual's ability to understand, recall, and manipulate knowledge, not the ability to supply the most popular answer. Boster points out that both approaches work. In addition, a combination of the two approaches could be the best of all. Because I have a high number of experts in my sample, which will at a disadvantage in consensus analysis, the alternative "wave" approach would allow a more balanced analysis of my consultants. I could keep the valuable idea of consensus while using methods more aligned with wave theory.

Chavez et al. (1995) measured intracultural or at least subcultural variation across two domains using free lists, frame substitution tests, and ranking. They compared perceived risk factors for breast and cervical cancer and their importance among 5 groups (Latinas, Mexican women, Salvadoran women, Anglo women, and physicians). They found that different groups had different models of risk and different patterning of those models. They were able to conclude that even in the same main culture, different subcultural groups have different understanding of knowledge. This study is an interesting model for my own research, since I am looking at different groups within Western culture with differing yet perhaps overlapping perceptions of health care. Especially informative are Chavez et al.'s methods. The women supplied their own risk factors (free list), and the rankings, frame substitutions, and pile sorts were based upon this data. The most interesting part of this study, to me, is the practice of having consultants generate their own lists (such as herbal remedies) as well as the uses, situations, and/or qualities of the items.

Limitations of Some Approaches

1. Potential Problems in Gathering Domain Information

Free lists reveal variation both within and among groups. The groups may be at whatever level you decide as long as you use the appropriate technique to separate/distinguish them. Since I am interested in intracultural variation among distinct subcultures (where I know consultant membership in advance) I compare the overall differences in list/domain content and size. Then I compare saliency, frequency, and presence/absence of items among my groups.

"Loose talk and the freedom of free lists"

Despite its utility, there are a number of problems with free list analysis. First and foremost, there is great variation in the salience of items within a domain by gender, occupation, and frequency of utilization of items within a domain. Another problem with using free lists is the "loose talk phenomenon" discovered by Gatewood (1983) in which people often know the names of things with which they are not truly familiar. Some consultants may have a long list, but that list may be quite shallow, with little knowledge about the items listed. By pairing a secondary free list and yes/no questions about use and recommendation to each plant given in the herbal remedy free list, I hoped to offset the problem of the loose talk phenomenon. A comparison of the size of free list size to 1) percent of items used, 2) percent of items recommended, and 3) length of uses for those remedies should show the comparative "shallowness" of knowledge among consultants. In addition to the loose talk phenomenon, consultants may simply make up things to appear more knowledgeable in front of me. This source of error may be difficult to discern in situations with sample populations utilizing knowledge from a variety of sources. As discussed earlier, the defining natures of inventions of tradition and revitalization movements make it very likely that unreferencable or vague information sources will be given. Because these sources are vague or not readily available for verification and assessment, it may be very difficult to discern which items were made up on the spot by creative and eager-to-impress consultants.

Pile sorts have both advantages and disadvantages. Pile sorts have the advantage of revealing the differences and similarities in how different consultants organize and relate items within the domain. You can also elicit consultant names and reasons for individual categorizations. Successive pile sorts therefore allow you to build individual taxonomies for each consultant in order to compare them. In addition to this, there are several other perceived advantages to pile sorts. Pile sorts are generally believed by anthropologists to be pleasant, easily understood, and quick for consultants. In addition, pile sorts generate a wealth of *direct* information about *why* certain groupings are made. The less constrained format that should allow a relaxed flow of information with consultants that may make them comfortable and talkative. Pile sort data is more complex to analyze quantitatively, however, and tend to be described in more qualitative terms.

Experts are too "expert" for pile sorting

The tradeoff for the complexity and difficulty in analyzing pile sorts is the richness of the information they provide on hierarchical relationships among items. Pile sorts, then, are particularly good for deriving an indirect data to construct a model of the classification of the items within a domain by the hierarchical relationships among items generated by successive pile sorts. However, there are problems with using pile sorts with some types of consultants. While perceived by anthropologists to be fun and easy for many consultants, pile sorts can be quite frustrating to experts for performance, professional, and cultural reasons. The frustration of experts may be explained by D'Andrade's (1987) wave theory of knowledge. Because experts are familiar enough with knowledge within their domain of expertise to manipulate it in a number of ways, they can construct several *alternate* ways to sort the items. Their frustration may result from a desire to understand *which* type of organization is requested. Pile sorts may be better suited to nonexperts and non-professional experts (i.e. those who are not professionally trained or practitioners in the domain).

My personal experience with interviewing experts provides more insight into expert frustration with pile sorting. Evidence for the wave theory explanation of experts frustration is found in the behavior of experts during pile sorting tasks. Experts have sufficient knowledge of all of the elements of their system that they continually ask "how" or "which way" of sorting is desired. Even though eager to be helpful, the expert has so many ways of manipulating the items that they take a long time to perform all of the possible sortings and become fatigued. Experts may experience frustration at both the seemingly endless task of multiple pile sorts and the difficulty in choosing just one way of organizing the items.

2. Potential Problems Limiting the Usefulness of the Cultural Consensus Model

Any analysis using the Cultural Consensus Model is vulnerable to error if the assumptions of the cultural consensus model are broken. There are several assumptions of cultural consensus modeling, given in Romney et al. The three most fundamental were discussed above. There are other assumptions in cultural consensus modeling that could cause problems when investigating intracultural diversity, however. First, the interview subject is assumed to be a situation where ethnographer does not know either how much each consultant knows about a cultural domain or the answers to the questions. One expects a correspondence between answers of consultants that is a function of the extent to which each answer is correlated with the cultural truth. This is what allows you to identify experts. Outliers are weighted less because it is assumed that they are not as knowledgeable or "correct" about a single, fixed true "answer" that should apply to all consultants.

Already, there are several problems to applying this model. Because I have consultants who have purposely chosen different traditions, I already know that there are various correct answers and that there will be outliers. The assumed homogeneity of knowledge and consultants is blatantly the opposite of what I am studying. The various groups I wish to study were chosen for their variety. In addition, experts by definition tend to know more and different knowledge than nonexperts. Because of the assumptions of consensus as "correctness" on items, experts are at a disadvantage in consensus analysis and frequently score very low (Boster 1987). By contrast, consultants who know only a few items of high ubiquity are scored as the most culturally competent. This is exactly the opposite of most of the goals of studies of expert knowledge.

Cultural consensus modeling goes on to assume consultants don't guess and are independent. If consultants are obtaining their knowledge from the same source (such as an influential book), they will not be independent. The consultants may share some values, but all of the groups don't share single belief system.

Summary

In conclusion, many issues need to be considered before choosing data collection techniques. The cultural appropriateness of the methods, the specific information needed to meet research objectives, and the optimum balance between maintaining rapport and efficiently gathering data should all be factors in the final structuring of the research design. Background research to generate initial research questions guides the rest of the project design. Participant observation and informal interviews helps the ethnographer to establish rapport with the people in the culture to be studied and helps him or her to write better questions and choose methods that will be appropriate. Collecting oral histories and personal narratives from consultants provides rich information about the culture in the words of the people being studied. More specific data can be collected on cultural domains of interest with free lists. While free listing seems to be a robust technique appropriate to most if not all populations, other followup methods using the lists generated should be chosen to suit what the data and the population being studied. A mixture of rankings, pile sorting, ratings, survey questions, and frame substitutions may be chosen as needed. In some populations, other methods of obtaining the organizational data should be utilized as an alternative to pile sorting in order to avoid offending consultants to whom it would be uncomfortable for cultural or professional reasons. Carefully weigh your need for data to meet research objectives with the needs and feelings of your consultants. Time spent in participant observation and discussion with consultants about their comfort level with interview tasks may reveal potential problem methods and solutions to your research problems.

Name ______________________________ Date ____________________

Assignments

Learning More About Ethnography, Part 2

In Chapter 2, you began an assignment to read and summarize an ethnography. This second part of the assignment is designed to help you *evaluate* that ethnography.

For Part 2 of the assignment:

1. Describe the methods used by the ethnographer.

2. List any quantitative methods used and data gathered by the ethnographer.

3. List any qualitative methods used and data gathered by the ethnographer?

4. What research questions did the ethnographer begin with? Were each of these answered? List the questions and the ethnographers answers for each.

5. Were the ethnographer's research questions revised? How?

6. Did the ethnographer have any problems with their original research strategy? Describe the problems and any solutions the ethnographer tried.

7. What new questions or hypotheses arise out of the fieldwork?

8. Do you think the ethnographer was successful in choosing methods to answer their research questions? Explain.

9. Finally, can you think of other methods or data you would have liked to have seen in this ethnography? Describe.

Name ____ Date ______________________

Choosing a Research Question and Approach

Look back to the listing assignments from Chapter 1. What type of methods are used in these interviews?

From your results, can you generate a research question about reenactors?

Question: ____

____

How can you answer your research question? Is the data available from the interview from Chapter 1? If so, what data are you going to use and how are you going to use it? If not, what data do you need and what method do you need to gather that data? Write your research plan.

____

____

____

____

____

____

____

____

Present your data and describe whether and how it answers your research question.

____

____

____

____

____

Part 2

Who Are They? The Reenactors

Society for Creative Anachronism

5

This chapter provides an overview of the SCA, or Society for Creative Anachronism, with special attention to their defining characteristics, a description of my fieldwork with the SCA, and analysis of how these reenactors compare to other types. The Society's archives contain very detailed histories of the SCA itself as well as most of its groups. I hope to illuminate finer points and idiosyncracies from another perspective to enlighten lay people about SCA reenactors. Many of the sub-groups within the SCA maintain their own websites in addition to the Society's pages. Very detailed information on etiquette, customs, rules, and governmental organization is provided by the society for those who wish to join or study them in more depth. This chapter is an introduction to the group with an ethnographic perspective. I hope that it will provide the curious with some insight and perhaps interest readers enough to prompt them to learn more about their local SCA chapter.

It all started with a May Day theme party in Berkeley, California in 1966. The founding event was a May 1st tournament, and though the SCA did not incorporate formally until 1968, this event is considered the beginning of SCA reenacting. The idea caught on, and soon the SCA had spread around California and to college campuses around the U.S. Before long, the SCA was more than a college phenomenon. The "Known World", as the SCA's society and organized groups are known, now consists of 19 kingdoms with over 30,000 members around the world. Though formal membership in the SCA numbers around 30,000, many more people "play", or attend events, without formally joining. In the groups I observed in Meridies and Calontir, a solid 10–20% of event attendees were not members, though many of these non-members said they intended to eventually join when they became more established in the society or had more money. Membership is required for the individual to hold office and receive some of the honors by which one acquires status and rank within the Society. An independent minority of attendees who are actively reenacting non-members said they simply liked to hang out, without the need to participate in "any bureaucracy" and "play as they pleased" without commitment. Non-members usually are asked to pay a few dollars more to participate in events, and seem to be fully welcome as long as they do so. The general atmosphere is one of inclusion and welcome to all, and a special effort is made to welcome those who seem particularly shy or awkward.

The SCA is a not-for-profit educational organization. The two distinct characteristics of the Society that make it a classic reenacting organization are both facets of time. First, it is the Society for Creative *Anachronism*. An **anachronism** is something out of time, and the SCA is a creative world of shared, interactive play and make-believe located in an idealized version of time. Second, the SCA period includes the time of the European Middle Ages up through the Renaissance. Generally, you can get away with anything ranging from ~400–1700 CE (Common Era). The boundaries of time and geography are sometimes stretched, however. The original focus of the group was the European Medieval period, but you can find many individuals and groups dedicated to cultures and characters from the edges of that genre. Byzantine, Arabic, and a variety of Asian cultures are represented, though in much smaller numbers than mainstream European reenactors. Vikings are particularly popular in the Midwest and

The Author, Kristina Hayen Hill, Catherine Chanidling at an SCA wedding.
Photo by Karol Chandler-Ezell

North central U.S. The Romans are popular in some areas for a variety of reasons, including climate and the popularity of movies like *Gladiator.* I must say, after a brutal day of fieldwork in humid, 102-degree Kansas summer weather, I once gladly traded in my period-authentic (yet very hot) kilts for the light and cool Roman toga and sandals from a smart merchant. As the temperature climbed, many others decided to "go Roman" just to get some relief from the heat.

The goal of the society is to creatively develop and portray personae from the SCA period, using period-correct artifacts in a friendly *gentle* social environment. I say creative and gentle because everyone is expected to act and be treated as *gentlefolk* and everyone is to be tolerated and welcomed as long as they behave in this courteous manner. Gentle forms of address and chivalrous, courtly behavior are expected. Again and again, you hear SCAdians tell you, "this is the Middle Ages as they should have been," which means that everyone behaves in a courtly and chivalrous manner.

Maps of SCA distribution can be seen through links at the society's official website (www.sca.org). The Known World is organized into Kingdoms, with the densest membership and activity in the U.S., Canada, the U.K., Australia, and anywhere in the world U.S. military bases are located. This is because the SCA is very popular among military personnel, especially the Navy and Air Force. If you look at maps of non-U.S. SCA groups, you can see that many of them center around U.S. military bases and universities. (See Table 5.1 for a list of SCA Kingdoms around the world.) As membership waxes or wanes over time and social alliances within the SCA's various local groups shifts, the exact borders of the kingdoms sometimes shift, much as they did in the historic middle ages. New kingdoms arise, breaking away from the edges of older ones or forming when a large kingdom divides.

Within kingdoms, local and regional chapters are organized into households, ridings, colleges, cantons, marches, shires, baronies, principalities and a variety of other groupings. The groups are ranked by number of members. Households are the small-

Table 5.1. SCA Kingdoms around the world. Nations and continents are in bold, states and territories in regular font.

SCA Kingdom	Mundane Geographic Location
Aethelmearc	**U.S.:** West Virginia, western and wentral Pennsylvania, western NewYork
Ansteorra	**U.S.:** Texas, Oklahoma
An Tir	**U.S.:** Oregon, Washington, northern Idaho **Canada:** British Columbia, Saskatchewan, Alberta
Artemisia	**U.S.:** Montana, Utah, western Wyoming and Colorado, southern Idaho
Atenveldt	**U.S.:** Arizona
Atlantia	**U.S.:** Maryland; District of Columbia; North Carolina; South Carolina; most of Virginia; Augusta, Georgia
Caid	**U.S.:** southern California, Hawaii, southern Nevada
Calontir	**U.S.:** Kansas, Missouri, Iowa, Nebraska, and northern Arkansas
Drachenwald	**Europe, Africa, Middle East Sweden, Austria, Germany, Israel, Italy, Finland, Netherlands, France, Ireland, Spain, South Africa, United Kingdom, Greece**
Ealdormere	**Canada:** Ontario
East	**U.S.:** Eastern New York, New Jersey, Delaware, Massachusetts, Connecticut, Rhode Island, Vermont, New Hampshire, Maine **Canada:** Newfoundland, Nova Scotia, New Brunswick, Quebec
Lochac	**Australia, New Zealand, Antarctic**
Meridies	**U.S.:** Alabama, Georgia, Tennessee, Louisiana, Mississippi, Arkansas, panhandle of Florida, part of Kentucky, part of Virginia
Midrealm	**U.S.:** Illinois, Indiana, part of Kentucky, Ohio, Michigan **Canada:** small part of Ontario
Northshield	**U.S.:** North Dakota, South Dakota, Minnesota, Wisconsin, upper peninsula of Michigan **Canada:** Manitoba and northwestern Ontario
Outlands	**U.S.:** New Mexico, eastern Colorado, eastern Wyoming, El Paso, Texas
Trimaris	**U.S.:** Florida (except western panhandle)
West	**U.S.:** northern California, northern Nevada, Alaska, **Far East: Japan, Korea**

est grouping, consisting of several friends sharing similar interests and led by a Lord and Lady. Members of a household tend to work and play together more frequently than they do with other members in their area, though sometimes households are formed as a local group in the absence of a nearby larger grouping. Large towns, smaller cities and/or universities often support colleges, cantons, or shires. Shires consist of several individuals, including a few households and/or other societies and groups. Cities are usually necessary to support a barony, with the modern cities of Tucson, Kansas City, St. Louis, and Austin all supporting baronies. Access to frequent societal activities is important, and thus suburbs or nearby cities surrounding these baronies often support their own shires and other groupings. A smaller core group often forms the social center for members—a few to a few dozen individuals that reenactors see and engage in social activities with frequently.

Two gentlewomen relax in their finery.
Copyright Jupiter Images.

Kingdoms are led by a king (usually) or queen and that person's consort. The Crown is won through prowess in combat during events called Crown Lists. The fighters in the kingdom compete in a tournament, with the winner becoming the Prince and heir apparent for a trial period (of 3-6 months) before ascending to the throne at Coronation. Though I use the male terms, females sometimes win. In that case, she becomes the Princess with her consort and then the Queen with her consort. Kingdoms are not seated in a particular town but rather with the current rulers. Different kingdoms have evolved fairly different cultures with very different flavors. Overall rules for all groups in all kingdoms of the SCA abide by the Corpora, a set of rules and guidelines adopted by the Society.

The smaller groups are often arranged in a nested hierarchy, though not always. In other words, though a shire is smaller than a barony which is smaller than a kingdom; the shire usually reports directly to the king's court and is not nested underneath a barony. The organization is feudal, with ceremonial rankings by group, but this is very much a method of organizing and arranging social events based on member population. The individual members are treated with the type of respect and given the rights one would expect in an egalitarian society. In anthropological terms, status is achieved through display of skill and dedication although the old titles used are revived from feudal, ascribed-status cultures. SCA kings and other lords are given respect for both their individual prowess and their offices, and the individuals holding those places must win their right to their titles in competition.

To Play

So what do SCA reenactors do? Like the other types of reenactors discussed, they select a time period that appeals to them. The time period is rather broad in the SCA compared to Civil War or even Renaissance Faire reenactors. Though most choose Western

European cultures as their focus, a variety of other options are available, including Asian, Mediterranean, and Near Eastern cultures as long as the time period rules are observed. They dress in clothing replicating the styles of the Middle Ages and Renaissance to socialize at a number of events including feasts, tournaments, wars, workshops, craft fairs, classes, and practices. While they are there, each portrays his or her "persona", a fictional person set into a historically feasible narrative background. In other words, they do not reenact actual historical figures. For instance, you cannot arrive at an SCA event and claim to be Henry VIII, one of his wives, or another particular person from history. SCA personae are historically feasible, however. The background, skills, clothing, artifacts, heraldic device, and name should match. Many SCA reenactors try out several personae before settling on a favorite. This favorite "real" persona can then be registered, going through a thorough vetting by the College of Arms in the SCA who check the persona for consistency and historical feasibility and ensure that it does not duplicate another member's persona. The names and heraldic devices for each registered persona must pass muster with the College of Arms.

To begin, most people encounter the SCA in two ways. First, they see SCA members out at play, either at a demonstration event or some sort of practice. Demonstration type events include reenacted demonstrations for the public such as fighting, dancing, music, archery, and crafts at local festivals, faires, and public events. For instance, my first encounter with the SCA was at a Zoo Days event when I was in high school. The SCA had a demonstration area alongside local craftsmen, clowns, merchants, and performers. As someone who both read a variety of science fiction and fantasy novels and loved history, I found them fascinating. Practices are also common ways for Mundanes (SCA folk call non-SCA either folk "mundanes" or "moderns" and refer to the non-SCA world as "the Mundane or modern World") to encounter and observe SCA reenactors. Fighter practice is commonly held in public parks and on college campuses, drawing in a trickle of interested parties who are fascinated by the activity. Archery practice requires a safer environment (because of all the flying projectile weapons) but also draws in passersby. Dance and music practice or demonstrations bring in still another type of interested party. The SCA recruits new members in this way much the same as other reenacting groups do. They had individuals who were very charismatic and eager to talk with outsiders about what the SCA does. It worked, and I begged my mom to let me go to a few events. The recruiters typically talk to interested parties in great detail, hang out for a while, let them try their hand at a few reenacting crafts or skills, and then arrange to contact them for follow-up information. This contact person (often known as the group's *hospitalier* or *chatelain*) usually helps the new recruit to begin generating a persona and helps them borrow garb (period-appropriate clothing) for their first event. This is the same pattern Civil War reenactors use, and it seems to be quite a successful way to bring in interested parties.

The second major way of recruiting new reenactors is through word of mouth. A reenactor tells a friend or acquaintance about their reenacting and invites them along. Since SCAdians really enjoy what they do, they often want friends to come and give it a try. In this case, the friend is usually the facilitator, though they often get assistance from SCA friends with the process of enculturating a newby.

So, how do you enculturate a new SCA reenactor? The willingness to come play is the first requirement. Playing the part is also important, and appearances matter. Often, someone will lend you clothing, called 'garb,' that is appropriate to the time period. Soon, though, you begin to make your own garb. One of the first and continuing activities that reenactors engage in is foraging (shopping) for materials and patterns to construct good garb. In this great search for garb, the other details are passed on: How do you act? How do you address people of various ranks? What do all these new terms mean? What's an event? What's a war? And, based on the clothing styles you like, what time period and geographic location are you going to choose for your persona? These are the sorts of rich enculturating processes that take place alongside the act of making garb together. Throughout the reenacting cultures, acquiring garb and other gear is one of the most central activities through which reenactors socialize and bond.

The newby often gets a starter persona with the help of his or her friends. As they become acclimated and have a chance to learn to do their own research, new reenactors begin to settle on the details for a long-term persona. Discussing persona and the factors pro and con for particular historical periods and cultures is a major social activity in the SCA. Many people take a few years to develop their main persona, which becomes their identity in the reenacting community. (That said, they often enjoy playing at different personae when the mood strikes.) SCA persona are different from Civil War and other battle/war-based reenactors in that the reenactors maintain a central, permanent persona. When referring to other reenactors, SCA reenactors use their SCA persona at most times. They also occasionally appear to have a mild form of personality disorder, as you'll hear them refer to their 'other self' in terms of their activities or history. This is important, for the SCA persona is both integrated into the reenactor and kept as an alter ego. The balancing of this reveals the function of this type of reenacting. The SCA persona is a personality over which the reenactor has control: it is a character whose name, history, background, talents, and personality can be created, edited, and refined over time. The reenactor owns it, and the persona can become real within SCA social settings once others recognize it, receiving awards and achieving social status. The persona is also *you and you would make yourself,* that you incorporate into a new you as you create it.

Think about the implications, particularly if you are frustrated or unhappy with your life and social environment as it is. With an alternate persona, you can visit another time and place as a person you enjoy being, in the company of others who are doing the same thing. This is why SCA reenactors call what they do "play." It is make-believe, and it is cooperative play that is socially constructed. The others agree to play by the rules, making the SCA, or "Knowne World", a place you can visit in company with your friends as the person you want to be. Far from being psychologically unhealthy, this allows a much-needed break from every life's stresses and pressures. Some people choose to escape in this way from lives that are unhappy, unsuccessful or otherwise unpleasant, others from lives that are happy or successful, yet full of pressure. When this happens, you often see inversion of status. For instance, people who have high-status daily (Mundane) lives often crave a persona which has a more leisurely pace of life. Surgeons, engineers, and a variety of other professionals often choose to portray simple "tavern wenches", smiths, or peasants. By contrast, reenactors with low status in the Mundane world often crave recognition and high status within the reenacting society. The role reversal is part of the therapeutic nature of the escapism.

What else is involved in entering the reenacting world? The new reenactor learns behaviors such as bowing, speaking gently, and using honorific terms for others. Jargon, slang, or specialized language for both one's time period and for the shared society of the SCA is learned. Garb, device, persona, and mundane are just the beginning. The proper forms of polite address for people of various positions is learned, though Milady and Milord (forms of My Lady My Lord) are good when the rank of the individual is unknown. In general, it is impossible to be too polite. Taboos and customs must be learned. For instance, the royal presence (the area around the King and Queen, Prince and Princess) is not an area one strolls across casually. Proper obeisance and respect must be shown. The archery and fighting fields are also sacrosanct for safety reasons. Children and new reenactors are taught immediately not to enter an area where fighting or weapons could be in play. This is particularly important, given that the archers use real bows and arrows that could be deadly even with blunted practice points. Heavily armored fighters often have impaired peripheral vision with their helms on, and though they use safety swords instead of raw metal blades, they could harm an unarmored, unpadded person. Though regalia and gear sometimes includes real knives, it is taboo to draw a blade without a loud "clear" and it is definitely taboo to threaten someone, even in play. Many events actually require that such blades be safely tied or secured so that they won't accidentally fall out or come lose. Rude or unchivalrous behavior is verboten and can result in social censure and even a request that the individual leave.

The Characters and Events

Where to start? There are many groups of interest within SCA reenacting. Fighters are probably the most noticeable. Men and women who are fighters must learn from a more experienced member how to safely participate in their chosen style of combat. While Jousting and horseback fighting do occur, they are comparatively rare in the SCA. Horses are expensive, and fighting on horseback is very dangerous, even with blunted weapons. You are much more likely to see Jousting and medieval combat on horseback at a Renaissance Faire, done by professionals. Most SCA fighters are 'sword' fighters on foot. I put sword in quotations because they actually tend to use boffer or boffle swords made of tape-wrapped rattan poles. These round swords do not cut, but deliver ample blunt force. Fighters are required to wear minimum safety gear, including a padded helm. Armor varies from padded leather to chain mail to plate metal breastplates and can be quite expensive. Fighter practice is often held weekly or biweekly, making it an easy activity to go observe. Non-fighters often go to fighter practice to watch the fighters and hang out, chatting with other reenactors. It is common to see several ladies embroidering or sewing on the sidelines, chatting with other reenactors during fighter practice. This provides a routine, frequent activity for socializing. Archery practice is similar to fighter practice, though archers and fighters are often different crowds.

Arts and Crafts people include several groups. Weavers and fabric makers often enjoy each other's company and have events and activities together. Skills range from embroidery, sewing, knitting, leatherworking, ceramics, smithing, jewelry-making, cooking, soapmaking, herbalism, brewing, calligraphy, and more. Most reenactors participate in several different Arts and Crafts skills as a part of learning more and enriching the reenacting experience. A great deal of appreciation and recognition amongst reenactors is shown for effort and/or excellence in crafts. Arts and Crafts includes lectures and workshops on historical topics, from eating customs of the Celts to period-appropriate underwear. Ongoing learning is very much a part of the historical and researching emphasis of reenactors. Awards and social rank within the Society are given for excellence in Arts and Crafts. Dancers and Musicians have practices and events and are recognized in much the same way. Though there are people who specialize or excel in these areas, all SCA reenactors are welcome to participate in these activities and most do to some extent.

Though demonstration events are held in the public eye, most SCA activities are private, focused on social activities for the reenactors with minimal intrusion from the Mundane world. Language, behavior, and dress are kept period when possible to emphasize that this is reenacting, not a Mundane activity. In this way, SCA activities are quite different from Renaissance Faires and many of the events of Civil War and other war reenactors. It is private, with the emphasis on shared play in a safe social environment, not a public exhibition.

Officers for the local groups have business meetings, which are often social as well. While business is handled, members enjoy period food, crafts, watching films, and the sharing of information. Meetings to work on garb or artifacts as a group are also common activities.

The leaders of a given group hold 'court', an activity in which the reenactors assemble and go over society business in a formal atmosphere. Schedules and announcements are made, awards are given, and individuals are recognized for their skill and/or work. Afterwards, there are often celebratory activities like music, dancing, and feasting. Reenactors often wear their best and most elaborate garb to court, as this is a formal environment for showing off one's finery.

Feasts are jolly events in which some of the reenactors prepare elaborate, period-authentic meals for the delight of the reenacting community. Reenactors from surrounding areas will often attend another group's feast, giving them an opportunity to socialize with each other. Participants are expected to bring their own feast gear (cutlery, plate, bowl, cup or tankard) as well as any elaborate beverages. Water and lemonade are often provided as part of the feast, with guests bringing mead, beer, ale, or other beverages of their choice if site appropriate and subject to mundane law. While appreciation of period-appropriate alcohol is a favorite adult pastime, great care is taken to make sure that minors do not drink alcohol at SCA-sponsored events. Indeed, though there are very adult activities in the later hours, great care is taken to keep any event with children present very family-friendly. Children's activities are often part of most events.

"Events" vary and include a variety of activities and are usually hosted by a local group with anyone invited. Battles, arts and crafts competitions or exhibitions, merchant faires, dances, archery competitions, and wars are common events. Several activities are often combined for an event. Most will include a feast in the evening, and at least some arts and crafts activities or educational activities are included in an event to make sure that everyone is able to entertain themselves.

A child kneels at Court to receive a commendation on a task well done.
Photo by Kristina Hayen.

Wars are some of the most spectacular events. Many last for one to two weeks, with the average being a Friday through the following Sunday. Reenactors will take vacation time to come out and experience this prolonged immersion experience. Wars are held in a secluded place, with an attempt to minimize Mundane intrusion. Multiple kingdoms participate, and they can get quite large. The largest and best known is the annual Pennsic War hosted in Pennsylvania by the Kingdom of Aethelmearc in August. (www.pennsicwar.org). The Estrella War hosted by Atenveldt (Arizona) in February, the Gulf Wars hosted by Kingdom Meridies in March, the Lilies War hosted by Calontir near Kansas City in June, and the Great Western War in Caid in October are the bigs interkingdom wars. Wars involve hundreds or thousands of reenactors simultaneously and offer a much deeper reenacting experience than shorter-term events.

Period weddings are another type of event thrown by individuals. Many reenactors enjoy the pomp and ceremony of the Middle Ages more than modern wedding trappings and elect to have Medieval or Renaissance Weddings. Often, most of the guests will also dress in period garb.

SCA Environment

The SCA social environment is different for different stages of life. It is family friendly, with an emphasis on providing a fun, safe, and educational environment for all ages. Many families reenact together, and there are special events for children. If they don't start from a reenacting family, high school is a common age for people to enter reenacting. Great care is taken to ensure their anxious parents that they will be safely and attentively cared for while they are at events.

College-aged reenactors are allowed more freedoms and able to participate in more risky or at least risqué behavior, though alcohol use is discouraged and actively prevented when possible for anyone underage. Adults from young to old find social groups with which to share a variety of interests, though most SCA reenactors I have observed are under sixty. As I've had opportunities to interact with the SCA at different stages of my life, I've observed that it is both the same world and a different world for reenactors at different stages of life.

Fieldwork Experience

Before I go into further detail about the characters, events and customs of the SCA, I should point out that this is the group in which I was able to immerse myself in the experience in the true style of participant observation during my dissertation fieldwork. Most of this fieldwork was in Calontir, though it built upon my experiences from high school and undergraduate college in the Kingdom of Meridies. My informants were mostly members of Meridies and Calontir, though some belonged to other kingdoms.

While in most contexts my interaction with SCA society was either informal or in the form of semi-structured interviews, I was able to conduct participant observation in one sample context. I was able to achieve the immersion which typifies participant observation and that allowed me to participate in activities alongside my sample population as "one of them" at Society of Creative Anachronism events. Unlike a place of business or even events designed to demonstrate to a regular audience, these events stress the need for everyone to "remain period" by dressing, speaking, and behaving in the agreed-upon form of "the modern middle ages." The boundary line between the performers and audience is not present, since everyone is participating in the same activity—group play. Since these events exist in a discrete time period and location, however, the researcher can "go there" and stay in the participant observation mode for a prolonged period of up to 10 days. This was a valuable way to establish rapport that is much more like standard anthropological fieldwork methods than other contexts.

During my fieldwork, I attended community activities and helped with tasks like food preparation, "riding the tents" during a thunderstorm, and dying cloth. I also attended ritual performances like "court"and "battles" as well as the classes on medieval and SCA-related topics that are at the core of this re-enactment-oriented community.

Over the course of the participant observation, I performed and experienced the activities that all "new" SCA members must complete. These included selecting a persona, creating a history and background for this persona, and then creating an appropriate wardrobe of "garb". I obtained assistance from a few key consultants with these tasks and they were gracious enough to invite me to several events, on shopping expeditions, and even into their homes to work together on my persona. The extensive

Details from medieval and Renaissance art are used as inspiration for reenacted rituals and artifacts. Copyright Jupiter Images.

literature research and labor involved in creating the various physical and nonphysical aspects of a persona are considered to be one of the most central and pleasurable aspects of this community. Since I mainly enjoyed 'daytripping' (playing without joining or formulating a permanent persona) when I was in high school and college, it was a novel experience to go through the enculturation that serious reenactors undergo.

Court proceedings in the Kingdom of Calontir. Photo by Kristina Hayen.

Most members trade services and skills in a sort of generalized or balanced reciprocity. I traded herbal information sources, recipes and preparations as my way of contributing to the group and reciprocating for the assistance and gifts offered to me by other members of the community. At the Lilies

War, a 10-day event near Kansas City, I was identified (by my key consultants) as an expert and contributed by volunteering to teach a class. My class drew many individuals who were interested in herbal remedies, and in this way I was able to obtain volunteers for interviews. In order to avoid "polluting" my sample pool, I taught a class on Mineral Herbalism. During this class I gave a history of Mineral Herbalism and showed my students how to make salt and clay-based products used in herbal remedies.

Later, several of the students from this class and their friends offered their encampment for trying the preparations, and to 'pay' me by giving interviews. (At prolonged SCA events, groups of friends or members of organizational groups such as households, shires, and baronies set up their pavilions near each other to form 'camps.') I arrived at their camp with my interview materials and a variety of mineral preparations demonstrated in class. I had noticed several common ailments during the course of the war, so I briefly left the camp to go to a nearby store to purchase supplies for larger quantities of salts, oatmeal, and other supplies to make remedies for the ladies. Everyone had sore feet from walking long distances, often in thin slippers or uncomfortable period shoes on uneven ground. The ladies' costumes revealed large expanses of shoulders and bosom that had painfully sunburned, and were suffering from sunburned faces from being outdoors all day every day despite wearing hats. In addition, several days without warm water in the campground showers and camping "in period style" while sweating in the heat of a Missouri/Kansas summer *while wearing full medieval costumes* had left many ladies with unfortunate skin conditions such as heat rash and acne. In my class, I had demonstrated cooling foot baths (with salt that would dissolve in cold water), facial masks, acne and blister plasters, and plasters for treating sunburn with my audience in mind. So, for this visit, I brought additional quantities so that everyone could enjoy sampling the remedies.

When I arrived at the camp, I discovered that the ladies had ordered 'their lords' (their husbands) to haul nearly 40 gallons of water over half a mile (uphill) and to set up an appropriate setting. This paraculturally—appropriate setting of open pavilions with rugs, pillows, stools, and chairs scattered on the ground for us to sit upon (and walk barefoot—a luxury in the camp) and tables for working. The ladies relaxed, chatted, and took turns being interviewed while they enjoyed foot baths, facials, and sunburn treatments. Everyone had brought something to contribute, from pots of honey (for snacks and to add into mud masks) and homemade mead to a bard with a great harp to play music for us. The men even fanned us while doing the hard work of attempting to heat the large pots of water at the campsite for facial steams and warm foot baths.

In addition to the ladies' party, I interviewed a key consultant in a public place near the classroom, then gave her a gift of perfume. She then showed off her perfume, and all of her friends wanted some. I offered consultants their selection from a basket of homemade preparations as a 'thank you for (your) valuable time.' In this setting/subculture, a homemade or herbal item is more enticing than a cash reward for interviews.

Most members of the community have sufficient income to participate in an expensive hobby (garb, paraphernalia, events are costly). What they crave is specialized knowledge of the culture with which they seek to connect. Herbal consumers wanted information from an expert. Practitioners appreciate shared knowledge as a sign of respect and evaluated my information as a judgment of my expertise. Sharing recipes and remedies was a way to make a place for myself within their society in a respectful way while contributing appreciated information. I was careful not to sell any of the remedies and so not compete with herbalists at the events who were attempting to sell remedies as part of their businesses.

I began this fieldwork searching for herbal practitioners, but what I discovered about reenactors and the differences among the different types of reenactors convinced me that there was a need for ethnographic research among SCA society. It was the realization of the importance of personae, alternate shared realities, and the sacred time in reenacting in the SCA which revealed how very adaptive a strategy reenacting is for modern Americans.

Name ______________________________ Date ____________________

Homework Assignment

Go to the Society for Creative Anachronism homepage at http://www.sca.org

How many official members does the SCA currently have?

How many kingdoms are there?

Get to Know Your Local Kingdom

What kingdom do *you* live in?________________ And what is your kingdom's website?

Is there a smaller SCA group in your area within that kingdom? What is it and how is it ruled?

How and when is your local kingdom's "king" chosen?

Who is the current ruler of your kingdom and how many SCA members does it have?

What events are scheduled near you in the near future?

Get to Know the SCA

Go to the SCADemo page (you can access it through the main www.sca.org page's information for newcomers or go directly at www.scademo.org

What sorts of activities are available to SCA members?

Why does the SCA promote participation in these activities?

How is this similar to the ethnographic methods and goals of participant observation?

What advice or information is provided to assist newcomers to fit in with SCA culture?

What behaviors and practices are emphasized?

What linguistic differences do you notice between everyday speech and writing and the script on the SCA pages?

What is the difference between a lady and a Lady? (and a lord and a Lord)? How are the two used differently in SCA speech?

Name ______________________________ Date ____________________

Understanding SCA Involvement

What are the basic assumptions of SCA involvement?

How does one acquire status in SCA society? Give several options.

What is the stated goal of SCA involvement?

Examine their published information on the websites.

Do you feel that this is an accurate description of their activities?

Describe how you think the function served by participating matches or differs from their stated goals.

Renaissance Faires

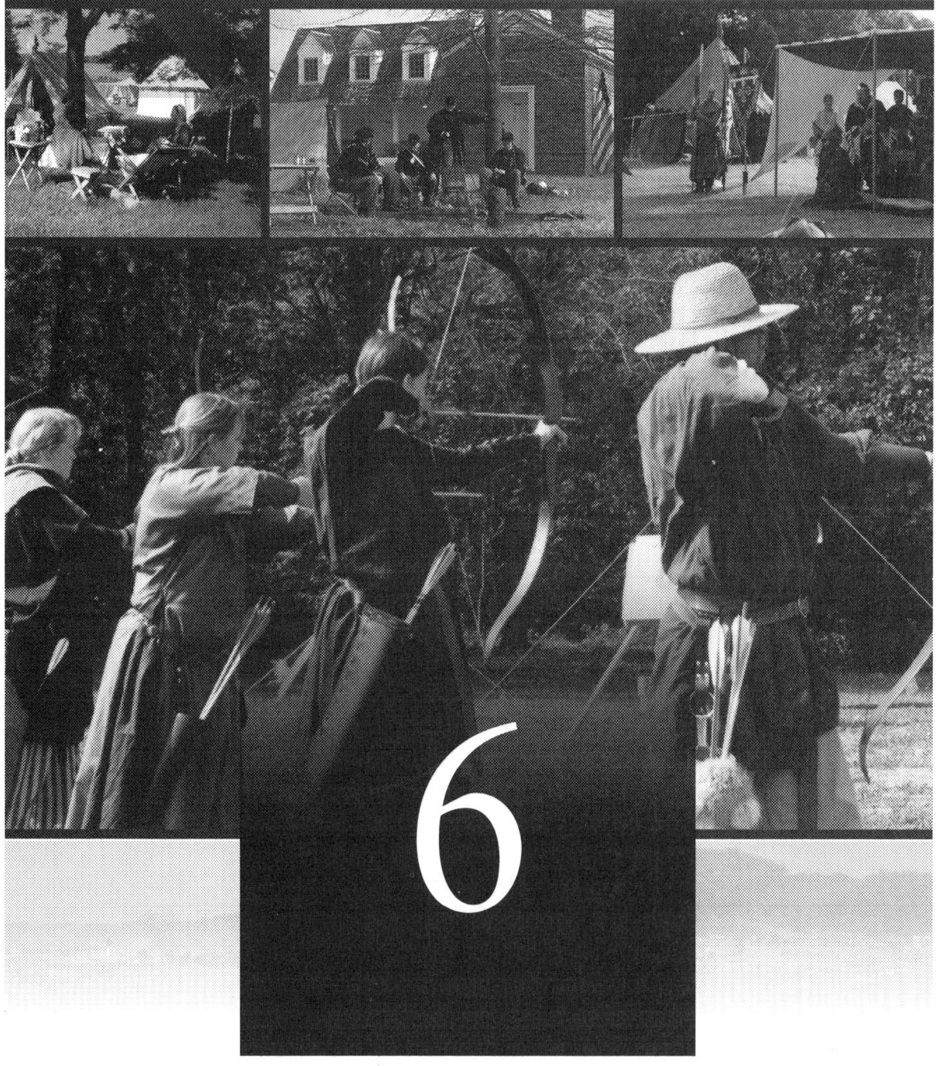

6

Renaissance Faires are festivals with a Renaissance Europe theme. The time period and genre of characters and artifacts is the usually focused particularly on the Tudor through Elizabethan periods. Usually called Ren Faires or simply Faires, these festivals are a mix of craft fair; theatrical or skill performances; and of course, historical reenactment. Faires are distinct from other forms of reenacting activities in that they are innately commercial ventures. While both SCA and Civil War reenactors put on some public events, they both focus the core of their social activities around private, all-reenactor events designed to exclude non-reenactors so as to have a more "pure" reenacting experience. Faires are designed to engage the public, with hired actors, performers, and Faire workers alongside merchants running businesses. The public are customers, paying an admission fee and enjoying the Faire as a recreational destination similar to a theme park. The atmosphere is created by the various Faire employees and set design, letting the visitor arrive with less necessary preparation. While visitors are encouraged to dress in a Renaissance style to better enjoy the experience, it is not demanded or even expected that most will do so. Instead, customers are necessary for these commercial ventures to be successful, with their money spent allowing the reenactors their chance to reenact.

Brant Johnson and Miranda Witherspoon at Texas Renaissance Festival, in character.
Photo by the Witherspoon Family.

Faires are similar to old local festivals in Europe dating back to at least the Middle Ages. These local festivals were often based upon important events like weddings, coronations, harvest, holidays, or other happy events. Traveling performers and merchants came together for these events. Locals prepared festival foods, often showcasing the bounty of a harvest or local and/or seasonal delicacies. People could show off their skills and accomplishments, competing for prices and recognition. These festivals or faires drew in a great number of people from the area, making them opportunities for socialization, courtship, and showing off one's finery. In short, faires were happy events full of revelry, eating great food, commerce, spectators, and fun clothes. With the Renaissance, the social atmosphere in Europe was much happier and open than it had been in the Dark Ages. Historical accounts record these events as happy, exciting times. Many of these festivals became annual events and continue as part of local European traditions to this day. Mardi Gras, Carnival, and numerous other festivals are descended from these events.

The important aspect of these festivals is something anthropologists call *sacred time.* Various public rituals are enacted, and the festival itself is an atmosphere where participants are in a liminal state much of the time. The festival atmosphere is one where the participants are freed from everyday social rules and inhibitions. The "betwixt and between" state of liminality Turner describes in his classic works on ritual are large-scale at festivals—but instead of progressing between life stages or ranks, festival participants are just engaging in a therapeutic escape from their everyday life and social environment. This is often emphasized by dramatic or outrageous costumes; masks; pranks; binging on food, alcohol, or other mind-altering substances; and other mischievous behavior not considered acceptable in everyday life. Often, role reversal is observed where people who normally have very low status are elevated while those with high status take on lower ranked roles. For instance, beggars, peasants, or other low-status individuals often become elevated to festival royalty. Today's Carnival Kings and beauty pageants at festivals are vestiges of this tradition. The May King and May Queen tradition observed in Great Britain is an example of local non-nobility being elevated to ritual royalty during a festival. Luckily, today's festival royalty don't face the risk of human sacrifice as they are reputed to have in festivals from Europe's Celtic past. By contrast, high status individuals or fine upstanding citizens often dress as fools or clowns and run about flouting social rules. The escape provided by the sacred time of a festival is therapeutic to both the individuals who participate and the community at large, allowing frustrations and social pressures to be released in a ritualized way. This feel of freedom and escapism from normal social roles is what is captured by today's Renaissance Faires.

The oldest Ren Faires in the United States date to 1963. Phyllis Patterson and the Living History Center in California are credited with the idea of modern Renaissance Pleasure Faires. The Living History Center, a non-profit organization, maintained a 1580s-era English village as a reenactment event designed to entertain and educate. The Renaissance Pleasure Faires started in San Bernadino and Novato, California in the Spring and Fall every year. These Faires sold food, crafts, and Tudor-Elizabethan reproductions while entertaining with actors and stage shows, and the LHC made an attempt to keep the actors and performances as historically-accurate as possible. The old LHC faires were purchased by the Renaissance Entertainment Corporation in 1993. REC began a professional joust group and reorganized the Faires to a mixed response among faire workers and reenactors. Today there are a few hundred Faires in the U.S. of various sizes. Some are small events that last a single weekend, while others run for a few months. The customers they draw vary from a few hundred to thousands annually. While most are still in the same Tudor-Elizabethan English genre, variants have arisen. Pirates and Faeries (aka Fairies) are very popular at most of the larger Faires and even have their own specialty Faires in some places now.

Though Faires are advertised locally, it's quite easy to find Faires across the country using the internet and such sites as www.renfaire.com, www.Renaissance-Faire.com, and many more easily accessed with a search engine. These same sites offer information about Faire culture, merchandise, and entertainment. Many have advertisements for a multitude of merchants selling faire-themed books, costumes, arts, crafts, music, and accessories.

While the Faires are commercial ventures, they also seek to share reenactment and a taste of living history with the public. Even though many of the merchants, artisans, performers, and administrators do make a salary (or at least recoup costs for their hobby); they do it for love of the genre and experience. The reenacting experience of Faire folk just happens to be different in nature from many other types of reenactors. One of the most telling ways to contrast Ren Faire and the seemingly-similar SCA experiences comes from my informants who had participated in both. SCA reenactors like to go to Ren Faires and even sometimes participate as demonstrators or organizers. I've been to a few Faires that were thrown by SCA groups. They were very short and small affairs lasting just one to two days, but the many of the reenactors dressed and acted differently because they were attempting to replicate a Faire environment. Mostly, SCA reenactors participate in Ren Faires that others organize. Many of them stand out, as they refuse to surrender their period authenticity even for a brief Faire experience and come as their medieval personae. (Which is NOT Elizabethan or Tudor English and therefore not the correct Faire period). A few of my Faire consultants called these SCAs (pronounced Skah's) gloomy Gusses and sighed over their refusal to "just have fun, it's a *Faire!*" It is interesting that SCA reenactors often call their reenacting experience play, yet have trouble exchanging their serious and authentic shared fantasy for the very public and openly fantastic play of the Faires. This is not true of all SCA reenactors, however. Many of them go to the Faire to "let my hair down and not worry about details!" A few of my consultants enjoyed dressing in their wilder garb, indulging in pirate, wizard, swashbuckler, or faerie princess costumes (their change of use, not mine) that they knew would be too flashy or ill-received at SCA events. In many ways, they treat the Faires much as authentic people across history have—as a time of inversion and play.

A pair of my SCA consultants who wanted a period wedding without all of the fuss of having to 'make everything from scratch, just right' for an SCA wedding actually went the shortcut and had their wedding at the Kansas City Renaissance Festival. Their garb was period appropriate for their SCA personae, as were many of their close friends. They found the Ren Faire to be a useful compromise, however, because their non-reenacting

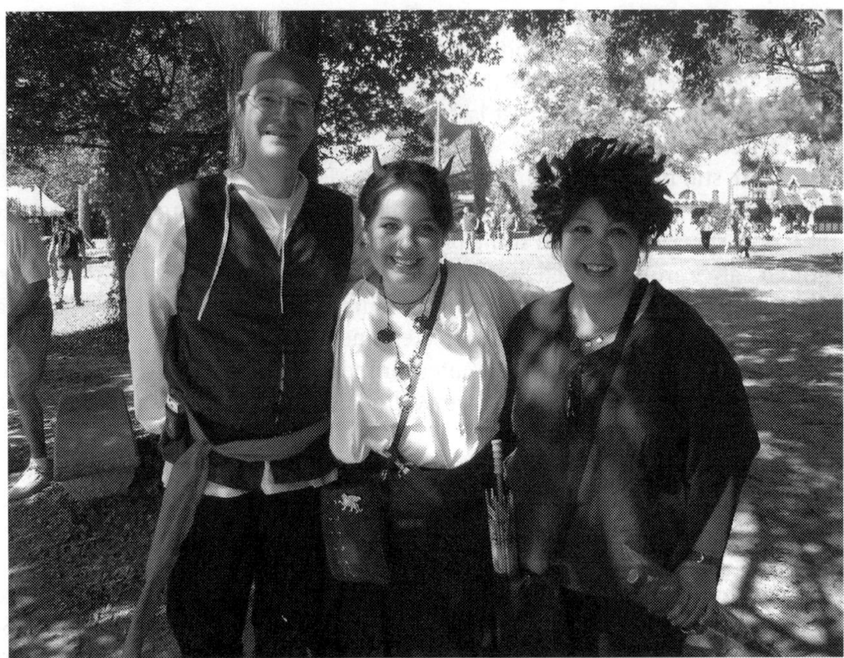

A family tradition of Ren Faire participation. Billy Cordova, Miranda Witherspoon, and Dr. Elizabeth Witherspoon at the Texas Renaissance Festival, 2006.
Photo by the Witherspoon Family.

family members were able to simply rent costumes from the Ren Faire. They had their period experience wedding with all of the details they wanted in decorations, music (Elizabethan lutes, flutes, and harps, of course), setting (a delightful reproduction Tudor chapel), and food (Ale, mead, turkey drumsticks, and a castle-shaped cake). The guests and family were "almost there on the time period" thanks to the assistance of the Faire's events office. The minister even dressed as an Elizabethan priest, and the parents of the groom and bride were able to let the event coordinator at the Faire fit them with elegant costumes for a very low rental cost. The event was fun for all, since guests received a free pass to the Faire to enjoy and "de-stress" all day. All in all, the festive atmosphere of the Faire let the newly formed extended family play at the Faire all day instead of focusing on the wedding details. They were very satisfied with their experience, and the guests had a delightful time. According to the Faire's event coordinator, Ren Faire weddings are very popular, and multiple weddings are often scheduled for each day of the Faire.

Now that we have discussed what Faires are not, it seems appropriate to describe the events themselves. Most of my consultants were merchants at the Faires, selling herbal remedies or magical items. Some of them participated in both Faires and SCA, but most Faire folk preferred the Faire. Their stated reasons were that they could reasonably expect to make a living, they preferred the festive atmosphere, and they liked the magical quality of Faires more. Being commercial ventures, Faires do draw people who are coming to an entertainment and cultural destination. The Faires are ephemeral—only lasting a short time, so those who love them often stock up or binge on Faire merchandise to "get them through the year", as a few of my consultants explained. The merchandise includes short-lived items like food, face painting, and flower wreaths. Other popular items are jewelry, accessories, artwork, crafts, and toiletries that can be enjoyed for a long time, reminding visitors of their fun. A great deal of costumes are sold, however, that are really only wearable for Faires and Halloween. Caught up in the excitement of the Faire, many customers buy costumes and put it on immediately so they can join into the reenacting experience instead of feeling separated by their obviously everyday, non-Faire appearance.

People who have enjoyed the Faires once often plan and prepare for their next visit by dressing in costumes. Some go into detail as elaborate, if not as historically accurate, as the garb SCA reenactors wear. Many Faires encourage a very historically authentic setting from their employees, though many do not. So, at most Faires the visitor will see a mixture including a few people in garb that would impress even a Stitch Counter with a multitude of polyester-satin enrobed princesses and gossamer faeries. Faeries,

Kristi Jones (left) and Miranda Witherspoon dressed as faeries at a Ren Faire wedding in Texas. *Photo by the Witherspoon Family.*

pirates, and wenches are very popular at Faires. Girls from toddler to middle age seem to enjoy wearing gauze fairy wings and wreaths in their hair. Boys and men alike seem to enjoy swaggering like pirates, though the small boys seem to indulge with plastic cutlasses more often while the men appreciate the bosom-exposing fashions of the ladies. Some Faires are held in tent cities while others have a variety of permanent structures in the Tudor or Elizabethan style. Many merchants have exciting setups such as tinkers' or gypsies' wagons to display their wares. There are multiple stages or entertainment areas. Some are small theaters where actors recreate Shakespeare-style plays. Moving through the crowds or on small performance areas, performers entertain with skits, improvisation, comedy, juggling, dancing, fire-eating, sword-swallowing, singing, music, and magic routines. Workers dressed and speaking in BFA (basic faire accent) man information booths and food vending. Basic Faire Accent and pronunciation, costuming, and acting are practiced by employees at the Faire, and the Faire administration often give their employees classes before the Faire begins.

The Faire structures are made of wood, stone, thatch, and stucco—or at least replicas of these period materials. The décor is as medieval as possible as well, with banners and ribbons fluttering in breezes heavy with the smells of food and sounds of music.

Jousting is one of the main attractions at most larger Faires. Indeed, armored knights and horses are prominent on advertisements for the Faires to play up this one-of-a-kind entertainment. A tourney field is maintained, with stands for the audience to view actual tournament-style jousting with lances, blunted swords or maces, armored knights, and large horses. Jousting is actually a competitive sport for many of the fighters, who make the rounds of numerous Faires much as rodeo riders compete on a circuit.

Renaissance Faires and the reenactors who inhabit them are quite different from Civil War and SCA reenactors. Despite this, there are some obvious similarities. Renaissance Faires do provide an environment for acting out a desired time-period fantasy. The fantasy part of the experience is both more open and more transparent, however. It is obviously fantasy given that supernatural creatures like witches, dragons, faeries, and theatrics are emphasized as the main themes of the Faires. That said, it is heavily populated people who are actors, consumerism, and entertainment. Other types of reenacting, such as that done in the SCA and Civil War genres, is also a fantasy, but it is heavily shrouded in attention to detail and reality. The very emphasis on achieving reality in personae, garb, and behavior by these types of reenactors is an attempt to pretend the fantasy is real. For, in their method acting, these reenactors want to achieve that period rush and escape into their shared reenacting fantasy. Faire reenactors are already working within a festival environment, where roles are already reversed and rules are already suspended. They do not have to push the reality of the experience to achieve sacred time, for they can purchase it when they enter the gate.

Name ______________________ Date ______________

Homework Assignment

Search for Renaissance Faires online

Look at the websites and advertisements for Renaissance Faires. What images are used?

____

____

____

What key words are used to entice audiences?

____

____

____

What are the stated goals of the Faires?

____

____

____

What events are scheduled near you in the near future?

____

____

____

Name ______________________________ Date ________________

Get to Know the Ren Faire

What sorts of activities or attractions are available to Ren Faire attendees?

____

____

____

What behaviors and practices are emphasized?

____

____

____

How do the Ren Faires compare to the SCA events described from the previous chapter?

____

____

____

What genres or characters are represented?

____

____

____

How do these differ from the Society and socially-based SCA events?

____

____

____

Civil War Reenactors

7

Civil War reenactors are the group with which I have spent the most time discussing, interacting, and pondering, yet have the least official fieldwork experience with. Let's start this chapter by discussing my interactions with this group. I will introduce you to some of the 'characters' I have met and I will also briefly touch on the history of the group. My purpose in this chapter is to do away with any preconceived notions you may have about this particular group being a bunch of redneck hillbillies or raving white supremacists stomping around in the woods with black powder rifles. As with each group we discuss, these are real people, with faults, flaws and fine points of their own. They are also enthusiastic, honorable, smart, well-read men and women from many cultural backgrounds who are committed to historical and cultural preservation. They love history, culture, and passing on traditions. As such, they have been incredibly helpful with the research and open to being ethnographic subjects and partners. As an anthropologist, it is rare to study a group so willing to share their culture and allow an outsider access. It is my hope that you will gain respect for these people and their love of historical heritage, just as I did.

When I was beginning my dissertation fieldwork as a graduate student at University of Missouri looking for traditional herbal practitioners, I initially observed and researched multiple types of reenactors, including the Civil War folks. I was surprised to note the regional differences between Missouri reenactment groups and those with which I had been familiar from central and Southern Arkansas. I observed Civil War reenactors in and around central Missouri and found that they were different in several ways. The first big surprise was all of the blue coats! In central and northern

Reenactors rest against a fence at Gettysburg.

Missouri, the Union soldiers were the good guys, and monuments stretched from Kansas City to St. Louis memorializing Union generals such as Sheridan, Sherman, and Grant—men who appeared as villains in such classics of southernism as *'Gone with the Wind"* and regional southern folklore. Yankees were the heroes to the east, north and west of me, yet in south-central Missouri, there were die-hard Confederate reenactors and even Missouri-German-immigrant militia reenactors.

Even more interesting, I noticed that the same men often unloading both Union and Confederate regalia—portraying either side as needed for the reenactment. And . . . that the reenactors were jovial and friendly with each other, even when they made Union vs. Confederate jokes. These men (and women . . . I had not realized the importance of women in Civil War reenacting before my fieldwork) enjoyed each other's company and were very peacefully and amicably reenacting the war known for its bitter divisiveness. The war in which brother fought brother is now reenacted by men who trade coats partway through the day in the interest of historical accuracy. The same old Civil War reenacting I had taken for granted during my childhood was much more complex than I had realized before I began observing them from an anthropological perspective. These historical reenactors had a culture not readily apparent to outsiders. I found that I, myself, had many pre-conceived ideas about Civil War reenactors that were naïve and simplistic.

My brother and sister are both history buffs, and we come from a family where regional history and family folklore are important topics. Both of my grandmothers were very interested in both family history and southern history surrounding the Civil War and reconstruction. My mother's family has unusually long generation spans, (my siblings and I are only the 8th generation since 1732 and my maternal grandmother's grandfather fought and was killed in the Civil War) and talking to my maternal grandmother Rose about her family's involvement in the war and the hard years that followed made the era seem much more immediate. This also strengthened my connections to both my grandmother and the war. Rose Beatrice Ashcraft Hanson Bunyard knew survivors of the war firsthand and could pass on the stories from her grandparents. My brother is particularly interested in history and genealogy, and has spent many long hours working on genealogy with both grandmothers. Coupled with his career as an officer in the U.S. Army, he is particularly well-read and knowledgeable about military history.

With this family background, I found myself talking about my research, and especially the reenactors, with my brother. Always helpful, he volunteered to go "check out" the reenactors he'd seen giving living history demonstrations at the museums and libraries in the Little Rock, Arkansas, area. His inquiries were met with cheerful helpfulness and warm invitations to participate. As he got to know them, he reported back that "These guys are pretty cool—very nice, and they really know their history!" He was hooked, and found himself a new hobby and group of friends in the process. He found that the reenactors he encountered enjoyed scholarly investigation of the Civil War, the military and American history in general—and they combined it with a social group in which they could "play hard" at history. As I was initiating my formal fieldwork with Ren Faire and SCA reenactor communities, my brother was beginning his own participant observation and enculturation with Civil War reenactors. He reported back his experiences, and I talked to him about my own similar experiences with SCA reenactors and Pow-Wow groups. The remarkable parallels in our experiences struck both of us as interesting, and we frequently compared notes.

We probably had our first really enlightening conversations about ethnographic method and anthropological fieldwork during this time. My brother immediately made the same connection I'd written in my own field notes. Reenactors are about participant observation and cooperative play. To take the analysis further, they are groups of participant observers who all agree to play together under a set of agreed-upon rules. As our parallel fieldwork progressed, I wrote in my notes that reenactors, except perhaps many of my Renaissance Faire consultants (more about that in the chapter on Ren Faire reenactors!) were really attempting to participant observe or "method act" their way into the emic perspective. We both encountered various versions of two phenomena: ***the period rush*** and ***escaping the everyday*** as goals of the reenactment process.

Escaping the everyday through reenacting is a common goal for reenactors. Again and again, reenactors describe reenacting as a form of therapeutic escapism that helps them to relieve stress. As with the SCA, many Civil War reenactors describe their chosen historical period as being more gracious, with people held to codes of honor and politeness. Male reenactors, in particular, like "treating ladies like ladies" and "being allowed to act the gentleman." Female reenactors report that, indeed, they find gentlemanly behavior amongst the male reenactors to be very appealing and feel very appreciated by this treatment.

What is "the period rush" for Civil War reenactors, though? It is much the same as the period rush described by SCA reenactors. For Civil War reenactors, they describe it as "being there, in the moment." They describe actually feeling the reality of the moment/time being reenacted. Much like SCA reenactors, they are able to lose their conscious awareness of themselves as their modern selves and feel like they are someone living through that event. They feel like they have captured the feeling, the emotion, and the experience of being part of the time. In so doing, they get a rush of exhilaration and bonding with their fellow reenactors as well as the actual people who originally experienced the events of the war.

This "period rush" is an interesting phenomenon that has been anthropologically described in other situations. For instance, a plethora of ritualistic activities are used in most cultures to achieve a **trance**—a state of consciousness where an individual or group has an experience where he or she loses touch with everyday reality. This transcendent experience can be an end to itself, leaving the individual feeling exhilarated, relieved of stress, and rejuvenated as a result. In religious ritual, the goal is to use this transcendent state to contact and communicate or at least commune with the supernatural. Many rituals are designed to give the individual a feeling of clarity by freeing them of everyday concerns or letting them obtain insight to a problem.

Public rituals guided by states, churches, and charismatic leaders create a mild trance-like effect called communitas. **Communitas** results in shared feelings of unity, bonding, and allegiance with others sharing the experience, with normal social structure,

Union Civil War Reenactors relax and chat next to a warm campfire. Soldier standing in right corner is Tom Ezell.
Photo by Steve Shore.

organization, and identity temporarily forgotten and replaced with the group bond (Crapo 2000). Skillful leaders can focus it to create feelings of brotherhood, loyalty, and nationalism while enacting rituals that relieve the public's stress, uncertainty, or anxiety. Even public sporting events are used to relieve stress and create a bonding experience between the audience members. The period rush seems to be a type of transcendent experience where the reenactors loosen the stresses or constraints of their real or daily persona and as a result gain feelings of rejuvenation, relaxation, and brotherhood. Interestingly, the basic training or initiation phases of most military groups purposefully include activities designed to induce just this experience as a way of increasing camaraderie among soldiers. This culture of brotherhood among warriors is an important part of honor codes for many military groups. Scott Atran (Glausiusz 2003) has described how Al Qaeda training programs are designed to create familial bonds among members by placing recruits in small units and subjecting them to training exercises that create strong bond. They then use this feeling of brotherhood to take advantage of **kin altruism**, so that members will readily give their lives for the good of their new, fictive kin.

It is in the participating, the actual enacting of historically-accurate activities, that reenactors are able to experience the period rush. Having several people work cooperatively together intensifies the experience and adds both the immediate experience of transcendence and communitas to the construction of long-term group bonding with fellow reenactors.

The War on Replay: History of Civil War Reenacting

Memorializing the war was common in the Union states following the war. Parades, memorial parks, statues, and holidays memorializing the war were common in both the North and South. Former Union soldiers formed the Grand Army of the Republic (GAR), with their descendants forming societies such as the Sons of Union Veterans of the Civil War (SUVCW) and the Auxiliary to the SUVCW as the years passed. The Grand Army of the Republic was particularly known for helping with charity, hospitals, and orphanages. Other Northern groups included the Loyal Legion, The Soldiers and Sailors National Union League, and other regimental or regional societies of veterans. The United Confederate Veterans formed in the South, with the United Daughters of the Confederacy, Children of the Confederacy, and the Sons of Confederate Veterans and numerous other smaller patriotic groups following over the years. Veterans from both sides of the war often participated in anniversary parades and public ceremonies. Though they also were social organizations, these groups did and continue to have a great interest in preserving and memorializing events and materials from the Civil War. A drive through many of the larger Civil War battlefield parks reveals multiple and impressive memorials, many of them donated by these groups. Countless other small historical markers and plaques commemorating Civil War events—especially battles and cemeteries—are scattered throughout the eastern and southern United States.

Veterans and these ancestor-based groups commemorated major (and even minor) battles with parades, speeches, and community events over the years. As the years passed, the war and its events were reinterpreted to suit current sociopolitical needs—particularly the heroic sacrifices necessary to forge a strong, unified, and "modern" or progressive country. From 1911–1915, fiftieth anniversaries of the Civil War were observed throughout the country with the admonition that forgetting them could result in a weaker, less patriotic country (*Harper's Weekly,* April 22, 1911, 4 cited in Franklin 1962).

The fiftieth anniversaries were observed by holding reunions at major battlefields like Bull Run, Antietam, Gettysburg, and Vicksburg. Indeed, these battlefields host some of the largest and most noticed (by the public) reenactments and memorial services today. The end of the semicentennial festivities and commemorations was somewhat sober, however, as World War I loomed. World War II cast a shadow over the 75th anniversaries of the Civil War, and as all but the very last few veterans had died by this time, little public ceremony or public attention marked these anniversaries.

The centennial anniversaries of the Civil War, however, did not compete with a world war and were lavishly celebrated. A historian writing at the time (John Hope Franklin), noted that "*One searches in vain for an event in our history that has been commemorated with the same intense and elaborate preparation that characterizes the Civil War centennial* (Franklin 1962, 103)" Among the preparations were national, state, and local Civil War Centennial Commissions, complete with budgets in the millions of dollars. Battlefields were set aside as parks, historical markers were erected, particularly in the former Confederacy. "*Impressive building shave been constructed to house the mementoes of the Confederate effort and to tell the story of the Lost Cause. Sham battles are being staged to stimulate the imagination and to encourage viewers to second-guess the outcome.*" (Franklin 1962, pg 104). Even during the centennial events, American responses to the commemorations were divided. While many threw themselves into the anniversary events with zeal and enthusiasm, others criticized the celebrations as juvenile and vulgar—a bizarre and inappropriate way to commemorate a national nightmare. Descendants of Americans from both sides of the war agreed, however: the horrors of the divisive Civil War were a national tragedy, but the war was the defining event, the shared nightmare, that forged a shared national identity for the United States. Confederate flags and paraphernalia were everywhere, but the people wielding them were *Americans,* intensely patriotic to the United States even while they glorified the dream of the Confederacy and the romance of the antebellum South.

After the dust settled on the Civil War Centennial events, we were left with a rich network of battlefield parks, museums, and memorials. Most of all, we were left with romantic, celebratory national memories of the war as the archetype of American heroism and historical legacy. Actual reenacting of the type that gave rise to today's reenacting traditions seems to have gotten started around the time of the early 1960s with the centennial anniversary of the war. Most of today's historical reenactors have little in common with the gaudy and often wildly inaccurate reenactments staged during the Civil War for public consumption. And, much like the "Cowboys and Indians" portrayed in pop culture and by Hollywood which have little to do with accurate portrayals of Native American Indians; Civil War-themed movies, novels, and television shows had little basis in historical accuracy. Historic reenactors often groan in dismay at these "Gone With the Wind" knockoffs and the Farbs they attract. How then, did the serious modern reenactors evolve if they did not come from this tradition?

Reenactors cross arms at Gettyburg, PA during a public reenactment.

Civil War reenactors who are intensely interested in historical accuracy and preservation are more a product of the living history movement that began with museums, state and national parks interpretation, and public education in the 1980s. Many of the first scholar reenactors began as museum tour guides, teachers, or historians who were attempting to 'liven up' history to make it more accessible for public education. According to Jay Anderson in *Time Machines: The World of Living History* (1984) and an earlier article in *American Quarterly* (1982), living history practitioners can be categorized into three groups. Anderson categorizes living history into museum professionals seeking a new way of educating, experimental archaeologists conducting research into past practices, and "history buffs" who reenact recreationally.

Museums began using living exhibits, or guides dressed up in historical garments, performing tasks or displaying skills from different time periods, as early as the 1890s in Europe. Colonial Williamsburg established live interpretation with historical reenactment in the U.S. when it opened in the 1920s and 30s. The popularity and success of Colonial Williamsburg established period reenactment and live interpretation as a gold standard for quality public history. "Living history" as a method of public education was adopted by the National Park Service in the 1960s and 1970s, as well as at several other historical or cultural institutions. These living history exhibits were quite different than stunt costumes or Hollywood-style entertainment. While the costumes and activities were designed to excite the public and capture their imagination, the goal was education. As a result, great care was taken to provide historically accurate presentations. Accurate reproduction sets, artifacts, clothing, even speech and behaviors were the goal. Living history reenactors attempted to "get into character" much as a method actor, by immersing themselves in detail. Living historians researched history, folklore, and technology to gain a more holistic understanding of their 'characters.' "Interpretation" was an important element at museums and historic sites as well. Park and museum interpreters were attempting to translate the perspective of people from a particular time period and context so that visitors could gain insight into what life would have been like in the past. The idea was that this would not only provide a richer, more fulfilling experience for the visitor, but would also help the public to form an emotional and personal link.

Historical reenactment can also be a research tool. Some questions about the abilities of past peoples and their technology can be tested by recreating them. Replica ships of various sorts have been constructed and sailed to test their seaworthiness and range. Replica weapons and tools can be used to test their effectiveness as well as what types of tool marks they would leave. In this way, archaeologists have been able to interpret tool marks on artifacts, bones, and buildings. Past agricultural, artistic, architectural, food preparation, and medical techniques have been tested in this way. When several techniques are proposed, reenacting the different techniques under controlled simulations allows scholars to test which leaves evidence that most closely matches archeological evidence. The newly revealed methods are then often shared with living history exhibits for public education.

Finally, Anderson categorizes the third type of living history practitioner as those who do it as 'play.' He includes the North-South Skirmish Association, a group that began reenacting Civil War battles in the 1950s among a list that includes other early reenactment groups like the American Mountain Men and the Society for Creative Anachronism in the 1960s and the Brigade of the American Revolution in the 1970s. Anderson does credit the popularity of living history participation as a recreational activity to escapism, but he emphasizes that it is healthy and beneficial recreation. It is play, but it is not juvenile. Instead, it is an opportunity for people to spend their leisure time in a social environment that better suits their preferences and personality.

Serious, or hardcore reenactors that attend several events a year, owe much of their culture to living history reenactors. Though there are many reenactors whose activities are purely recreational without a great deal of scholarly investment, these tend to be the reenactors who attend the occasional public event recreating a large battle. Hardcore reenactors invest a great deal of their time in research, public education, and interaction among other reenactors.

Today's reenactors frequently overlap into more than one of Anderson's categories. His recreational living history practitioners are much more cavalier about historical accuracy than the bulk of today's reenactors. In the parlance of serious Civil War reenactors, they sound like **FARBS.** The term 'Farbs' has a few different translations, some kinder than others. "Far be it from authentic" is the most common, though many gentlemanly reenactors will offer up a polite "Far be it from me to question his attempts." "Fast and Researchless Buying" and a few much ruder translations exist as well, though most of the gentlemen I interviewed were far too gentlemanly to repeat such things in front of a lady or to treat their fellows with disrespect. On a different note, Farb is sometimes reputed to derive from a German slang term referring to a carnival-goer or clown. Unless one of the first users of the term is found, we may never know the exact origins. The meaning, however, is clear among serious reenactors. That said, what is a Farb? To be accused of being a Farb means that your gear, clothing, behaviors, etc . . . are NOT PERIOD. I type this in all caps to emphasize the seriousness of this charge. To not be historically-accurate to the time period being reenacted violates the whole point of historical reenacting. If you are 'not period' you are not doing your part in joining the others in the right frame. You clash, you might jar others from the shared reality of the reenactment. Great effort is expended to enjoy the ambiance of shared play. A Farb who shows up with sneakers, blue jeans, a polyester jacket, or an Ipod can ruin the mood for everyone. And maintaining that mood, that shared reality, is the way that reenactors find that period rush together. Not all reenactors are hostile to Farbs and are genuinely accepting to anyone who wants to honestly join in, regardless of their ability to invest in a complete set of gear. Farbs probably do most closely resemble the earliest of Civil War reenactors in many ways as old veterans and their sons, daughters, and grandchildren dressed in their old gear or in home-made copies of uniforms and dresses to participate in anniversary commemorations of the war. Costume balls in the South held by the Sons of Confederate Veterans or the United Daughters of the Confederacy were much more Farb than most of today's serious historical reenactments.

So the question is, are Farbs bad? To the serious Stitch Counter (see below), Farbs are treated with great disdain and efforts are made to reform, control, or exclude them from events they might "ruin" for the serious. Most reenactors are fairly gentlemanly about them, agreeing that they have their place and the right to reenact as they choose. So-called Farbs are often descendants of war veterans and may be members of local historical groups. They often carry influence and can be quite beneficial to the cause of preservation. Though they like "showy spectacles" for the public to observe and do like to get dressed up in very showy period costumes, they are also generous and interested purveyors of local cultural preservation. They are more likely to be behind events such as balls, parades, and publicly-viewed "staged" reenactments. These events do reach the public, recruit new reenactors, and most of all—raise money to preserve historic sites. Farbs have a very important part in reenactor society, even if they are quite different in other ways from the other reenactors.

On the opposite end of the spectrum of Civil War reenactors are Stitch Counters. **Stitch Counters** are found in all types of historical reenacting, though they are frequently called 'Authenticity Nazis' in the S.C.A. A Stitch Counter does exactly what the name implies and more. He or she wants to see the inner seams and hems of garments to inspect the stitches. Were the stitches made in the appropriate style to the time period? What type of thread was used? What about the weave of the fabric? Cut of the pattern? The dyes used? Stitch Counters demand period perfection. They purchase or create patterns from actual historical garments. They closely inspect historical documents. I have met many who spin wool, weave fabric, and dye fabric in a historically-accurate manner. Buttons and belt buckles made from original molds (or duplicates made through reverse molds created from an authentic artifact) are a hot item on eBay and other reenacting mercantiles. If they can't manufacture materials from scratch, they will often get as close as possible and treat those materials to achieve an end product as close as possible to an accurate-appearing reproduction. Stitch Counters are chasing the fine details or authenticity through their artifacts, and this quest helps them to get "that period feel." They are the 'hardcore' reenactors that are beyond the casual description of 'history buffs.' The degree of detail they pursue and the sheer amount of knowledge they acquire in their quest begs the question: are they amateurs? Professional historians can definitely say they are amateurs by definition because they usually do not have formal degrees in history. Anthropologically, however, there are different categories that can be applied. Expert and Novice, or non-expert, are categories used for cultural knowledge domains. In the domain of their historical period, many reenactors are definitely experts, regardless of whether they have formal degrees in history or costume design. They have a great deal of specialized knowledge and are acknowledged as experts by their peers.

Most reenactors fall somewhere in the middle of the spectrum between Farbs and Stitch Counters. Sometimes called **Mainstreamers**, they do strive for historical accuracy and invest a great deal of time into their gear, but no one fears they will crack up if they discover a piece of synthetic material amongst someone's gear. 'History buffs' though they may be, most of these mainstream reenactors also have a great deal of expertise and are very involved in scholarly study of Civil War history, costumes, customs, and artifacts. That, in fact, leads us to the next topic: Just what do Civil War reenactors do?

What Do Civil War Reenactors Do?

In general, most Civil War reenactors spend a great deal of time doing research. They read histories, diaries, books, and newspapers from the Civil War era and the surrounding years. They read histories written about the Civil War after the fact. They study clothing patterns, technical diagrams or machinery, tools, and technology. They try to learn what people ate and how, their customs, their practices, their perspectives. In short, they try to learn as much ethnographic information as possible about the time period. They often write up reports to share with other reenactors through their newsletters or at meetings. Best of all, this research and hard homework is considered fun! Reenactors' research is a part of a social learning atmosphere. Sharing and seeking knowledge gives them a medium for interaction, cooperation, and reciprocity. Social status among other reenactors can be gained through scholarly prowess and/or skills at period technology.

Outside of formal social events or meetings, reenactors talk on the phone, hang out and chat, and interact via the internet. Research and the accompanying discussions in which reenactors share what they know and discuss their knowledge makes up the heart of the social component of reenacting. Being part of a reenacting community involves a great deal of socialization. This is probably the first misconception to dispel. Common negative comments about reenactors include "Get a life", "get out more", and "grow up." Reenactors do "have a life" and do "get out more". They have busy social schedules that are much more "grown up" than their detractors guess.

This social activity ranges from solitary research activities to group interactive activities. Individuals share what they have learned with others in the group (and often on the internet through newsletters and websites) through reports, summaries, talks, and demonstrations. New recruits are mentored by more experienced reenactors to help them learn reenactor customs as well as the technical knowledge to do living history. Group meetings often include historical lectures, the sharing of new information, and discussions of how to help with local, regional, and national historic preservation. Reenactors are often members of several organizations dedicated to history, battlefield preservation, and education. They will volunteer to put on living history demonstrations at local libraries, schools, cemeteries, monuments, festivals, museums, and parks. They will often work as extras for local tourism films and photos. They will reach directly into their pockets to make donations to preserve and maintain historic sites. The battle reenactments that catch the public eye are usually held to raise money and awareness for maintenance and preservation of parks and memorials. They physically clean up trash and debris in old cemeteries and hold public memorials. When they are offered a fee for reenacting (as in the case of movies or television shows), the groups will often agree upon a suitable project to which they donate the proceeds. In short, reenactors tend to be very civic minded, contributing time, effort, and money to protecting cultural heritage without compensation.

In living history demonstrations, reenactors dress and act as a person from the Civil War would have, yet interact with the public. They answer questions, show their gear, and show how things worked. Spectators to the museum, school, park or other event often want to see and touch their clothing or gear up close. Often, they have food or drink samples or works in progress to show manufacturing skills. They talk, telling stories and trying bring the past to life in a way that static displays do not. Often, Civil War reenactors are invited by museums and schools, working in cooperation with them to improve public turnout and satisfaction. Seeing "real" people and things from the Civil War brings it to life for people, especially children.

One thing that frequently surprises people is that many African Americans are involved in Civil War reenacting. This shouldn't be surprising, given the importance of the war to African American history as well as American history in general. The movie *Glory* brought African American contributions to the Union Army into the public mind, and real reenactors played many of the extras in that movie. African Americans also reenact as Confederate soldiers, for many African Americans were on both sides, both voluntarily and non-voluntarily. Though some soldiers were ex-slaves or escaped slaves, many were freeborn Northerners. Not all African Americans fighting on the Confederate side were conscripted slaves, though. Some were fighting for their homes willingly. The role of African Americans in the Civil War is a complex and fascinating topic, and that many men and women are exploring through reenacting. Racism in any form is seriously taboo in the reenacting community, and most groups prominently display prohibitions on any form of white supremacy or degradation of anyone based on their race. Tolerance and balancing both sides is often enhanced by having reenactors change sides and play Union one day, Confederate the next. Despite playing at a bitter civil war, reenactors are actually very friendly and agreeable with each other.

Reenactors also reenact events and practices from the Civil War. They cook, sew, manufacture, sing, and dance. Garments are very important for reenacting. While many purchase their clothing and gear, creating clothing is a very popular pastime among reenactors. Males and females will both work together to make costumes. My mother was quite tickled that my brother came to her for sewing lessons. He and his buddies acquired period patterns and all worked together to make their uniforms for an upcoming event. They started with period-correct cloth (no polyester, please). They searched out the correct types of fabric, some of it mail-ordered from merchants specializing in historically-accurate fabrics and dyes. They cut the patterns (a nerve-wracking business when that precious fabric is $70 a yard or more), pieced them, and sewed. They were very proud of their seams and the cut and fit of their coats. It took tremendous effort to get all of the details right, and the experience created a social bond among the men who worked together. Such sewing parties and similar meetings to work on artifacts and practice maneuvers are common social events.

Reenactors study antifacts preserved from the Civil War for detail.

Females also reenact the Civil War. Though some do battlefield reenactment, many of them reenact civilians and medical personnel. Women do sometimes reenact as soldiers. Most of them work hard to "pass as boys" as would have been necessary during the war. Female reenactors usually choose personae that are either local women or the wives and daughters of soldiers. They cook for the soldiers, nurse the wounded, bring water, and attend the all-important celebratory balls at battle reenactments. Though they are outnumbered by the males, female Civil War reenactors are a very important part of the society.

Civilian reenactors are common as well. Civilian roles include non-combatants such as local townspeople, government officials, merchants, and medical practitioners. The merchants are actually merchants selling specialized goods to reenactors. Part of the fun of a reenactment is shopping through an assortment of buttons, belt buckles, weapons, cutlery, fabrics, canteens, inkwells, lockets, tents, sabers. . . . You name it. The sheer variety of period merchandise at reenactments and through online merchants is staggering. Merchants sell gear and wardrobes in a range of authenticity from Flashy Farb to Stitch Counter perfection for the enthusiastic reenactor. They also sell food.

Period fare is an important part of the reenactment experience. Soldiers will attempt to eat historically-accurate meals and drinks when reenacting to truly capture that authentic feeling. A great deal of research goes into what was actually available at a given battle or time for both Union and Confederate troops. General consensus is that Yankees did eat better most of the time, with more reliable supply lines and the greater resources of the North, especially toward the end of the war. Great pride is taken in scrounging up foraged food and replicating the humble diet of the Confederate troops, however. Some reenactment coordinators use a sense of historical humor when provisioning the troops—such as providing the soldiers with chickens . . . live chickens that they must catch. The provision boxes often contain a historically-accurate assortment. Reenactor are left to use their ingenuity and equipment (period only, please) to Iron Chef some meals for their troops with their period provisions. If the fare is miserable, it adds to the experience, but it is often a matter of great pride to provide a delicious campfire feast from humble ingredients after a hard day of fighting.

The authenticity of the gear comes into play with environmental conditions. Soldiers sleep on the ground, with a blanket and perhaps a small tent. Whether it is cold, hot, mosquito-y, raining, sleeting, or lovely; they endure as the soldiers did. I am told, however that there is a limit. My brother told of one reenactment where they set up camp by the water's edge on a lovely site. Just as the park rangers left, they mentioned that the gator population had really been on the rise in recent years. As twilight fell, nervous reenactors watched for the gleam of alligator eyes and jumped at each splash or plop from the water. Daylight found most of them sleeping in the cabs or beds of their trucks. After all, wouldn't a real soldier have had the sense to take shelter from gators? Abandoned barns or churches on reenactment sites, park benches, old church pews, merchants' tables, and in one case a demonstrator's coffin have all served as shelter in howling thunderstorms. Despite their efforts, reenactors often endure miserable conditions and awaken to fight in the morning just as the real soldiers did. Enduring miserable weather, mud, and blistered feet from authentic footwear all add to the authenticity of the experience. The serious reenactor is on a quest to understand what it would have been like for the real person at that time. The physical reality actually helps to break out of the modern self and experience the subjective state of mind and body.

The War on Replay

Finally, reenactors go out and recreate battles from the Civil War. They do their best, given the limitations of numbers and park regulations, to retrace the movements and events of battles. Gettysburg, Vicksburg, Antietam, Shiloh . . . and many many more battles are reenacted. Some are recreated annually, others every few years or even once a decade. Particular anniversaries are usually larger events, though this varies. The public can usually come out for one or two "battle displays" on a Saturday with a possible repeat showing on Sunday afternoon. They spread out, sometimes on bleachers, often on lawn chairs and blankets they have brought, and photograph the big battles. Civilian reenactors often have living history demonstrations nearby that cater to the public as well. Often there is a nearby museum or historical park with their displays. People can make donations that go to the maintenance of the memorials or museums. The whole event is a public festival. That's the reenactment the public sees.

The real event experience, however, goes on behind the scenes for the reenactors. They arrive Friday night from their jobs and set up camp. The campsites are usually off in the fields, away from the town or museum. Campsites are kept as authentic as possible, and the reenactors form up into their assigned groups, getting to know each other. They visit with each other, cook dinner, and generally socialize in a period environment. The reenactors' camps are liminal—separating them from their everyday lives and letting them enter that period environment so they can get into the period mood together. They form up and move around in the morning, often playing at a few skirmishes or other events—all out of sight of the modern audience. When they do reenact, they have often managed to become involved enough in the play that they are not jarred out of the period rush by the spectators. It allows them to stay in character and enjoy the event despite the outsiders.

This is not to say that they never ham it up for the public. They do enjoy putting on a good show, both for the spectators and for each other. The art of dying is important. Though it's important to "die" in a way that's visually impressive to the public, it's also important to die in a comfortable place. Contorted in the bright noonday sun may look great, but the guy's got to hold that pose. "The smart soldier finds a nice shady tree with a good view and dies comfortably settled." The boom of the blanks in their guns and cannons is always good for spectacle, and a good "rebel yell" is important to the thrill of combat. These aren't completely for show. The noise, the smoke, the rush of running through the woods or across the field in full battle engagement is a huge part of the rush. It's a way to get caught up in the excitement and fear, and it's the reason they actually reenact battles instead of just marching around town squares. In fact, several battle reenactments do not have a public component. They are purely for the reenactors. Even in these reenactments, great care is taken to use blanks or safe cartridges and practice strict gun safety. The guns are real, but the bullets are not and the safeties are on. Nobody wants to accidentally harm another reenactor. These are bloodless battles.

Of course, I'd be remiss if I forgot to mention the balls. Most battle reenactments have a ball on Saturday night. It gives a chance for males and females to interact, for relaxed partying, and different garments. Reenactors who enjoy it replicate the music, and most of them try to dance and socialize. The gentlemen get to be gentlemen for the ladies, and a sense of the graciousness of the antebellum period is recaptured for a night. Even the grumpier super-masculine guys confess to enjoying the balls occasionally, though they say they only do it "for the ladies."

Why This War?

Why do so many people choose to reenact this particular war? What is so attractive, so salient, about the American Civil War? When I ask reenactors, they say that it speaks to them—pulls at their imagination. It is salient to them in a way that is both immediate and distantly romantic. The Civil War or "War Between the States" is immediate to many Americans in a variety of ways. In the comparatively short cultural heritage of the United States, the Civil War stands out. It was a unifying experience because the whole country suffered through it, regardless of what side they favored. It was a national tragedy and many historians claim that it was the event from which American nationalism and our sense of ourselves emerged. The Civil War (and in the U.S. it is "*The Civil War*") is a concrete event which forms the focus of U.S. history in a way that the strung out and less coherent periods of North American colonization and the American Revolutionary War are not. Colonial America is a garbled cluster of Pilgrims, Thanksgiving, and the Salem Witch Trials to most Americans. The Revolutionary War, the French & Indian Wars, and the War of 1812 are jumbled together in our national memory as events of the Eastern seaboard including George Washington chopping down cherry trees, crossing rivers in the cold, and lots of men in wigs (not to be confused with Whigs and Tories). Mention *The Civil War,* however, and we have photographs. We see images of men and women who look real to us, though their dress and hairstyles are different. We know Gettysburg, Slavery, Lincoln, the Confederacy, and the burning of Atlanta. Most of all, we remember the battles and the romance of the Antebellum South. Physically, the Civil War is all around us, at least those in the Eastern and Midwestern portions of the U.S., because this war happened on home soil. The Southern U.S. endured not only the war but long decades of Reconstruction. Battlefield parks, historical markers, museum exhibits, and local festivals all bring us fleeting yet persistent contact with the past not just in the East, but in Tennessee, in Missouri, and Louisiana. It was a momentous event that happened here—under our feet.

The Civil War is immediately recognizable in our collective imaginations, though we differ in our interpretations of events and their meaning. At the same time, the Civil War is the romantic past. Times were different then. *We,* Americans, were different then. The Civil War offers the reenactor both enough historical legacy and contact into today's world that it can be reenacted and enough cultural distance to let one escape into a different world. It is fantasy yet has substance and meat that can satisfy a need to connect in a way that is very real and fulfilling.

Name ________________________ Date ______________

Assignments

Cultural Impact and Maintenance of Folklore

How big of an impact does the Civil War have on your family? You may need to ask a relative like a grandparent or parent to answer these questions.

1. Have you ever been to a Civil War reenactment or living history demonstration? If yes, what did you think about it?
2. Are there any Civil War historical markers or sites near your home? If you can't recall, you can check local Chambers of Commerce, libraries, or City Museums. Describe the sites below.
3. Are there any reenactments or living history exhibitions featuring the Civil War near your home? Who sponsors and participates in these?
4. A. Do you have an ancestor who was in the Civil War? What do you know about this person? How did you learn this?

   B. Call or visit an older relative and ask them what they know about your ancestors' involvement in the Civil War. Ask how they feel about this family character (proud, embarrassed, etc . . .) and why.
5. On what "side" or sides did your ancestors participate? How do you think this affects family feeling about the war? (Non-combatants count, too.)
6. How do you feel about your family's Civil War involvement? (If your family does not have a historical connection, please answer how you feel about the war as an "outsider.")
7. How do you think cultural factors such as religion, awareness of racial sensibilities, modernization, and the current political climate affect perception of the Civil War and people's maintenance of associated folklore?
8. Which "side" do you think has more active reenactors, Union, or Confederate? Why do you think this?

Get to Know Your Local Reenactors

There are several different Civil War interest groups. The oldest of these are based upon memorialization or ancestral connection. In this assignment, you will learn how to distinguish reenactors from other Civil War interest groups.

Find your local reenactment groups or Civil War memorial associations.

Name ______________________________ Date ____________________

Memorial/Ancestry-Related Associations

Confederacy

1. Go to the official website for Sons of Confederate Veterans (SCV).
   Write down their url ______________________________
   Where are the nearest SCV groups to you?

   Look at their news postings. In what sorts of activities are they involved?

2. Go to the official website for the United Daughters of the Confederacy (UDC).

   Write down their url ______________________________

   Where are the nearest UDC groups, or chapters?

   Look at their news postings. In what sorts of activities are they involved?

Union

3. What was the Grand Army of the Republic? Was there a group near your home?

4. Go to the official Sons of Union Veterans of the Civil War (SUVCW) website.

   Write down their url ______________________________

   Where are the nearest groups?

   Look at their news postings. In what sorts of activities are they involved?

5. Go to the official site for the Auxiliary to the SUVCW.

   Write down their url ______________________________

   Where are the nearest groups?

   Look at their news postings. In what sorts of activities are they involved?

Name ______________________________ Date ____________________

Reenactment-Focused Groups

Groups that are primarily focused on reenactment and living history are quite different from those such as the SCV or SUVCW that are based upon ancestral connections. Reenactment-focused groups can readily be distinguished with a quick review of their websites and newsletters.

1. Look for other Civil War groups that focus on reenactment and living history. Find at least three. You must find at least one group that reenacts Confederate troops and at least one that reenacts Union troops. Try to find a group that has people reenacting *both* sides (Yes, there are many reenactors that readily portray personae from either side, as needed).

   For each, list:

   The url for their website:

   The name of their group

   What group or groups they portray in reenactments or living history demonstrations:

   These groups almost always post a mission statement, creed, or policy statement. Write down this statement for each group:

2. Compare and Contrast: How are the reenactment-focused groups different from the SCV, UDC, and SUVCW groups? You can compare and contrast reenactment-focused groups from ancestral/memorial groups by answering the following questions about each:

   What images appear on the group's website as illustrations?

   What criteria do they have for membership?

   What topics are covered in their websites and/or newsletters? (Write down the names and topics of the articles and news)

   How do their activities compare?

   If they do fundraising, for what do they raise money?

   If they do volunteer work, what do they do?

Name ______________________ Date ______________

3. Based on this information, how do the groups compare?

Which group is closer to your original perception of Civil War reenactors?

4. Does this information change your perception of Civil War reenactors? If so, in what way?

Interview Practice: What Do Reenactors Actually Do?

For this exercise, you will practice interviewing a reenactor. You can usually locate reenactors that are willing to discuss what they do at either a reenactment or a local living history exhibit (reenactors are easy to find at local libraries and museums for these events.) You may also contact a reenactor through one of the websites you studied for the exercise above.

(You may notice that you will be using a variety of question types, remember that you will learn more if you let the consultant talk and even answer questions before you ask them or in a different order. You can always go back and re-ask or ask the consultant to clarify the answer to a question. Interrupting him/her, though, to keep rigidly to your interview sheet will only alienate your consultant, so resist the urge and go with the flow.)

Record the following information about your reenactor consultant:

Name: ______________ Age: ______ Occupation: __________

Where or how you located your consultant for interview: ______________

____

Ask the Following Questions

What is the name of the reenactment group or groups to which you belong?

____

____

____

Name ______________________________ Date ____________________

Are you a member of any other historical or related groups?

____

____

____

Which was the first reenactment group you became involved with?

____

____

Please tell me how you become involved with reenacting.

____

____

____

What do you most like about your current reenactment group?

____

____

____

Name ______________________________ Date ____________________

Can you tell me how much time you spend in each of the following reenactment-related activities? When done, go back and ask the consultant to rank the activities.

Activities	Time spent (hours/month)	Rank by importance
Reenacting battles		
Living history demonstrations		
Practicing skills		
Research and reading		
Garb/costume construction		
Manufacture of other artifacts		
Shopping/browsing for materials		
Conversation with other reenactors		
Meetings/ administrative or organization planning		
Educational or charitable work		
Other . . .		
Other . . .		

What do you think you get out of reenacting?

____

____

____

What is the thing about reenactors that you would most like non-reenactors to learn?

____

____

____

Conclusions

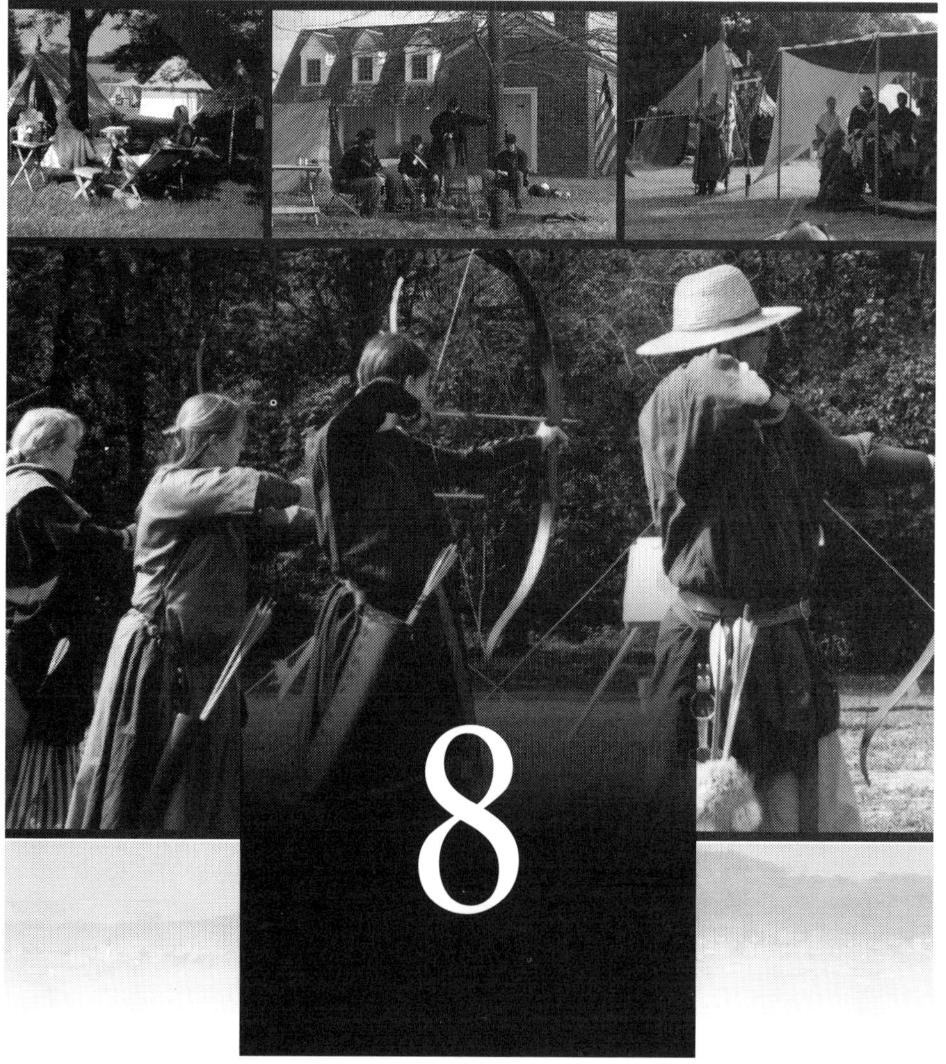

8

Different Types of Reenactors

Though there are many types of reenactors, this book focuses on three prevalent genres of historical reenactors in the U.S. While all share similarities, each is unique. Civil War reenactors and SCA reenactors are more similar in behavior, goals, and method even though Ren Faire reenactors overlap into the SCA genre. The SCA is the most private reenacting experience, with most activities among the reenactors taking place out of the public eye. Civil War reenactors balance public demonstration with the need for private and authentic experiences in their quest to preserve historic sites and cultural memory with the American people. Faire reenactors openly embrace public spectacle and consumerism.

The period rush reenactors seek is achieved in different ways. Faire reenactors create a festival atmosphere, where the cultural setting of a festival experience, role reversal, and loosening of normal social constraints creates the escapist benefits for both the reenactors and their spectators. Faire reenactors are processual actors, memorizing a script, accent, and relying on the freeing experience of being an exhibitionist performer. They revel in their festival characters in the loosened social environment of the Faire world. SCA reenactors are seeking a time long ago in a place far, far away. Though many reenactors know they have ancestors from medieval Europe, most of them do not know the details of this heritage and are far removed from it in a cultural sense. They must recreate or invent a historical envelope with the help of others in their society. They are drawn to a vague and misty past that is different enough to be both fantastic and a very real alternative to their daily lives. The very distance of the SCA genre is what makes it an escape destination. Because they construct detailed, long-lived, and very personalized personae, they carry the past within themselves. The SCA reenactor can alternate between parallel realities, moving into their paraculture when they need to escape daily social pressures or interact with fellow reenactors. Civil War reenactors are different from either of the other types in that they are standing rooted on their genre. While medieval Europe is a fairy tale land from the past, American land and culture is saturated with the Civil War. Especially in

Carnival and Mardi Gras are classic examples of role reversal and the use of masks or costumes to be free of everyday social constrictions. *Copyright Jupiter Images.*

the South and many of the Eastern U.S., Civil War reenactors physically encounter battlefields, memorials, and important historic sites from the Civil War. They are raised on family legacies that are close enough to be personal—grandparents tell them the stories of their grandparents . . . close enough for deep personal meaning and fulfillment, but just far enough for fantasy and the excitement of an alternate reality.

Faire reenactors rely on the fun of dance, games, and recreational activities for excitement. Civil War and SCA reenactors (along with some Faire artisans) can feel a sense of connection to their heritage and a sense of accomplishment by mastering skills and technology from their past. These sorts of activities are important cores to reenacting society, offering activities for bonding as well as the chance for achieved status amongst their new communities not based on mundane world status. The living history and method acting approach of the quest for period authenticity lets reenactors be deeply involved in both their escapism and their new society. Immersion and intense, climactic experience such as battle reenactments allow the reenactors to get lost in the moment and enter a different world. When they return to their mundane world, they often find that they are less stressed and better able to cope with the social pressures that await them there.

Given the nature of reenacting, what is its function? In the previous chapters, we reviewed misconceptions and stereotypes about reenactors. They are accused of being childish or psychologically deficient because role playing is considered an immature

Photo by Steve Shore.

form of play in our society. Adults are expected to maintain mainstream social roles. What the popularity of reenacting shows us, however, is that some adults need a break from their mainstream social roles. Dissociative psychological disorders occur when an individual loses the ability to integrate social variables and reality and dissociate from their social role involuntarily. Often, these occur when an individual has faced extreme social pressure. Inability to escape from social pressure in a healthy way through other methods could actually cause a person to break psychologically. Cultures are full of methods for mediating that stress. Festivals, rituals, and communal activities can ameliorate stress and let the individual feel a sense of communitas with others in a way that vents social pressures. Insufficient escapist or moderating behaviors can result in individuals accumulating too much stress, and therefore cause anxiety and unhappiness.

Reenacting allows people to spend time in a different social role, one that is chosen and constructed to the preferences and tastes of the individual. The time period or status of the characters being reenacted gives variety and allows an escape to an alternate social experience. It is play, but it is not immature. It uses the mechanisms of play, ritual, and festival behavior to achieve a therapeutic response. Reenacting is an adaptive method for coping with the pressures of our current social environment. More importantly, reenacting groups participate in several behaviors designed to create and strengthen social bonds among others, creating a social network. The reenactor not only finds a method of venting pressure but also creates a new social group in which they have alternate ways of achieving status and interacting in a healthy way. In conclusion, historical reenactors have discovered how to integrate hobby, play, and ritualized behavior into a folk psychological therapy. They create a new social environment where they are happy and successful, then use that social network to buffer the excessive stresses of their mundane lives. Paracultures are parallel social environments that can absorb today's overload of stress. Paracultural behavior, from reenacting to extreme forms of hobby enthusiasm, could be symptoms of a need in our culture for mechanisms to deal with the stress our social roles place on individuals.

Masks and costumes for festivals are often fantastic or surreal to add to the sense of altered time. *Copyright Jupiter Images.*

Name ______________________________ Date ____________________

Homework Assignments

What are some of the stresses of today's life that could lead to a need for reenacting or social release?

____

____

____

What types of stresses are often blamed for the onset of dissociative disorders?

____

____

____

What are some types of dissociative disorders and the stressors that are believed to be causative?

____

____

____

What are examples of customs or behaviors that are designed to alleviate stress? Describe the custom and how it can relieve social pressure.

____

____

____

Name ______________________________ Date ____________________

How are Mardi Gras and Carnival examples of the concepts of sacred time and role reversal?

____

____

____

Propose a strategy for integrating the idea of moderating social pressures into an escapist activity. Describe your strategy and how it would be beneficial. Be sure to discuss the pros and cons of this strategy.

____

____

____

References

Abate, Frank R.
1997 The Oxford Desk Dictionary and Thesaurus. Oxford University Press, USA; American Edition.

Adler, Margot
1986 *Drawing Down the Moon* (1981, rev. ed. 1986). Penguin Books, London.

Agnew, Vanessa
2004 Introduction: What is Reenactment? *Criticism 46*:327–339.

Anderson, Jay
1984 *Time Machines : The World of Living History. AASLH American Assn for State and Local History.*
1982 Living History: simulating everyday life in living museums. *American Quarterly 34*:290–306.

Barnett, Homer G.
1953 Innovation: the Basis of Cultural Change. New York: McGraw Hill.
1957 Indian Shakers: A Messianic Cult of the Pacific Northwest. Carbondale, Illinois: Southern Illinois University Press.

Bernard, H. Russell
1995 Research Methods in Anthropology: Qualitative and Quantitative Approaches, 2nd edition. Alta Mira Press, Walnut Creek.

Black Confederates: The Forgotten Men in Gray. 2002. Desert Rose Productions. Documentary film by Stan Armstrong

Borgatti, S.
1998 ANTHROPAC 4.95. Analytic Technologies, Natick, MA.
1999 Elicitation techniques for cultural domain analysis, chapter 1 in The Ethnographic Toolkit, Schensul, Jean and Margaret Weeks (eds.) Sage Publications, Newbury Park, California. at http://www.analytictech.com/borgatti/etk.htm

Boster, James S.
1986 Exchange of varieties and information between Aguaruna manioc cultivators. American Anthropologist 88:428–436.
1987 Introduction. American Behavioral Scientist 31:150–162.
1994 The successive pile sort. Cultural Anthropology Methods Journal 6(2): 11–12.

Boster, James and Susan C. Weller
1990 Cognitive and contextual variation in hot-cold classification. American Anthropologist 91:171–179.

Briggs, Charles L.
1996 The politics of discursive authority in research on the "invention of tradition". Cultural Anthropology 11(4): 435–469.

Canton, Cathy
1999 Reenactors in the Parks: A study of external revolutionary war reenactment activity at national parks. Report for the 225th Anniversary of the American Revolution Planning Committee. NPS. Pdf available online at http://kingsownpatriots.org/parks.html

Chandler-Ezell, Karol
2003 The Modern Herbal Synthesis: An ethnobotanical investigation of the emergence and function of herbal medicine in the revitalization of American healthcare. (Ph.D. Dissertation) University of Missouri, Columbia, MO.

Chavez, Leo R. , F. Allan Hubbell, Juliet M. McMullin, Rebecca G. Martinez and Shiraz I.

Connerton, Paul
1989 How societies remember. Cambridge: Cambridge University Press.

Cullen, Jim
1995 *The Civil War in Popular Culture: A Reusable Past.* Smithsonian Institution Press, Washington, D.C.

D'Andrade, Roy
1987 A folk model of the mind. *In.* Cultural Models in Language and

Thought (editors Dorothy C. Holland and Naomi Quinn.) Cambridge University Press.

Gatewood, J. B.
1983 Loose talk: Linguistic competence and recognition ability. American Anthropologist 85:378–86.

Garro, Linda C.
1986 Intracultural variation in folk medical knowledge: a comparison between curers and noncurers. American Anthropologist 88:351–370.

Glassberg, David
1986 *Time Machines: The World of Living History* by Jay Anderson. Review. *American Quarterly 38*(2): 305–310.

Glausiusz, Josie
2003 The Surprises of Suicide Terrorism. *Discover,* October 2003, pp. 21–22.

Glory 1989 Tristar Pictures. Film directed by Edward Zwick.

Golphin, Vincent F.A.
1998 Black Confederates have their own lesson to teach. About . . . *Time Magazine* (November 1998).

Handler, Richard, and William Saxton
1988 Dyssimulation: Reflexivity, narrative, and the quest for authenticity in "living history". *Cultural Anthropology,* Vol. 3, No. 3 (Aug., 1988), pp. 242–260

Haviland, William A.
1997 Anthropology. Fort Worth, Texas: Harcourt Brace College Publishers.

Hobsbawn, Eric, and Terence Ranger, eds.
1983 The Invention of Tradition. Cambridge: Cambridge University Press.

Hopman, Ellen Evert and Lawrence Bond
1996 People of the Earth: The New Pagans Speak Out. Inner Traditions Press, London.

Hutton, Ronald
2000 The Triumph of the Moon: A History of Modern Pagan Witchcraft. Oxford: Oxford University Press.

Jacobsen, James E.
1997 The Civil War in Popular Culture: A Reusable Past. *Civil War History 43:*

Jorgensen, Joseph G.
1972 The Sun Dance Religion: Power for the Powerless. Chicago, Illinois: The University of Chicago Press.

Keesing, Felix M.
1953 Culture Change: An Analysis and Bibliography of Anthropological Sources. Stanford, California: Stanford University Press.

Kehoe, Alice Beck
1989 The Ghost Dance: Ethnohistory and Revitalization. Fort Worth, Texas: Holt, Rinehart, and Winston.

Kimbrough, David L.
1995 Taking Up Serpents: Snake Handlers of Eastern Kentucky. Chapel Hill, North Carolina: The University of North Carolina Press.

La Barre, Weston
1938 The Peyote Cult. Norman, Oklahoma: University of Oklahoma Press.
1962 They Shall Take Up Serpents: Psychology of the Southern Snake-Handling Cult. Minneapolis, Minnesota: University of Minnesota Press.
1970 The Ghost Dance: Origins of Religion. Garden City, New York: Doubleday & Company, Inc.

Linton, Ralph
1943 Nativistic movements. American Anthropologist 45:230–240.

Lowie, Robert H.
1914 Ceremonialism in North America. *In* Lowie's Selected Papers in Anthropology, published 1960. C. Du Bois, ed. Pp. 336–364. Berkeley, California: University of California Press.

McCurdy, David W., James P. Spradley, and Dianna J. Shandy
2005 The Cultural Experience: Ethnography in Complex Society. Waveland Press, Inc. Long Grove, Illinois.

McLoughlin, William G.
1984 Cherokees and Missionaries, 1789–1839. New Haven, Connecticut: Yale University Press.

1986 Cherokee Renascence in the New Republic. Princeton, New Jersey: Princeton University Press.

1994 The Cherokees and Christianity, 1794–1870: Essays on Acculturation and Cultural Persistence. Athens, Georgia: The University of Georgia Press.

Milne, K.

1993 Fighting a very civil Civil War. *New Statesman & Society* August 20, 1993: pp.12–13.

Mishra.

1995 Structure and meaning in models of breast and cervical cancer risk factors: a comparison of perceptions among Latinas, Anglo women, and physicians. Medical Anthropology Quarterly 9(1):40–74.

Mooney, James

1891 The Sacred Formulas of the Cherokees (revised and republished 1929 as "The Swimmer Manuscript: Cherokee Sacred Formulas & Medicinal Prescriptions"). Washington, D. C.: Bureau of American Ethnology.

1896 The Ghost-Dance Religion and the Sioux Outbreak of 1890. Chicago, Illinois: 1965 edition abridged, with an Introduction by Anthony F. C. Wallace. The University of Chicago Press.

Native Americans of The Civil War 2006. Desert Rose Productions. Documentary film by Stan Armstrong.

Nolan, Justin M. and Michael C. Robbins

1997 A measure of dichotomous category bias in free listing tasks. Cultural Anthropology Methods Journal 9 (3):8–12

Peterson, Kristen

2000 Black Confederates: Slaves or soldiers? Las Vegas Sun (August 19, 2000).

Rauschenberger, S. L., and S. J. Lynn

1995 Fantasy proneness, DSM-III-R Axis I Psychology, and Dissociation. *Journal of Abnormal Psychology 104*:373–380.

Romney, A. Kimball, Susan C. Weller and William Batchelder

1986 Culture as consensus: a theory of culture and informant accuracy. American Anthropologist 88:313–339.

Ryan, Gery, Justin M. Nolan, and Stanley Yoder

1999 Successive free listing: Using multiple free lists to generate explanatory models. In press. Currently available at website: http://showme.missouri.edu/~anthgr/Classes/ANTH377/377.htm

Stanton, Cathy

2000 Review: Battle Road 2000. *The Journal of American History 87* (3): 992–995.

Strauss, Mitchell D.

2003 Identity Construction Among Confederate Civil War Reenactors: A Study of Dress, Stage Props, and Discourse. *Clothing and Textiles Research Journal 21*:149–161.

Strauss, Mitchell D.

2003 Identity Construction Among Confederate Civil War Reenactors: A Study of Dress, Stage Props, and Discourse. *Clothing and Textiles Research Journal 21*:149–161.

Thrupp, Sylvia L., ed.

1962 Millenial Dreams in Action: Essays in Comparative Study. The Hague, Netherlands: Mouton & Co.

Trevor-Roper, Hugh

1983 The Invention of Tradition: The highland tradition of Scotland, *in* Hobsbawn, Eric, and Terence Ranger, eds. *The Invention of Tradition.* Cambridge: Cambridge University Press, pp. 15–42.

Turner, Rory

1988 Bloodless Battles: The Civil War Reenacted. *The Drama Review* 34 (4): 123–136.

Tylor, Edward B.

1871 Primitive Culture. 1:424–425.

Vener, A.M. and C. R. Hoffer

1965 Adolescent orientations to clothing. *In* M.E. Roach & J.B. Eicher (Eds.)

Dress, adornment and the social order (pp.76–81). New York: John Wiley.

Wallace, Anthony F. C.

1956 Revitalization movements. American Anthropologist 58:264–281.

1966 Religion: An Anthropological View. New York: Random House.

1970 Culture and Personality. New York: Random House.

Wallis, Wilson D.

1943 Messiahs: Their Role in Civilization. Washington: American Council on Public Affairs.

Weller, Susan C.

1983 New data on intracultural variability: the hot-cold concept of medicine and illness. Human Organizations 42:249–257.

1984 Consistency and consensus among informants: disease concepts in a rural Mexican village. American Anthropologist 86:966–975.

1987 Shared knowledge, intracultural variation and knowledge aggregation. American Behavioral Scientist 31:178–193.

1998 Structural interviewing and questionnaire construction. *In* Handbook of Methods in Cultural Anthropology. H.R. Bernard, ed. Pp. 365–410.

Weller, Susan C. and A. Kimball Romney

1988 Systematic Data Collection. Sage Publications. Newbury Park, California.

Whitehead, Alfred North

1926 Religion in the Making. Cleveland, Ohio: Meridian Books, The World Publishing Co.

Young, James C.

1981 Medical Choice in a Mexican Village. Rutgers University Press, New Brunswick, N.J.

Young, James C. and Linda C. Garro

1982 Variation in the choice of treatment in two Mexican communities. Social Science & Medicine 16: 1453–1465.

Online resources and Reading Material:

Human Relations Area Files http://www.yale.edu/hraf.htm, database

The Authentic Campaigner, http://www.authentic-campaigner.com , newsletter

The Watchdog http://www.watchdogreview.com, newsletter

Civil War Historian magazine

North & South, a peer-reviewed magazine

Renaissance magazine, http://www.renaissancemagazine.com

The Society for Creative Anachronism, Inc. www.sca.org

The Knowne World Handbook, Society for Creative Anachronism

Tournaments Illuminated, quarterly magazine of the Society for Creative Anachronism

Compleat Anachronist, quarterly pamphlet of the Society for Creative Anachronism